D0943224

Berta

Elmer

Drawn Together

Drawn Together

...in art
...in love
...in friendships

The Biography of Caldecott Award-winning Authors
Berta and Elmer Hader

by Sybilla Avery Cook

Concordia University Publishing
Portland, Oregon

FIRST EDITION
Typography and Cover Design by Lori A. McKee.
Title Font by Judy Waller.

———————————————

Cook, Sybilla Avery, 1930-
Drawn together in art... in love... in friendships : The biography
of Caldecott award-winning authors Berta and Elmer Hader / Sybilla
Cook Avery.

p. cm.
Summary: The biography of Berta (Hoerner) and Elmer Hader, authors
and illustrators; winners of the 1949 Caldecott Medal for
The Big Snow published by Macmillan.

Includes bibliographic references and index.

Hader, Berta. 2. Hader, Elmer, 1889-1973. 3. Illustrators--United States--
Biography. 4. Artists--United States--Biography. I. Cook, Sybilla Avery,
1930-.

NC975.5.H33 C66 2015   741.6—dc23

Library of Congress Control Number: 2015949915
ISBN (10) 1-934961-06-X
ISBN (13) 978-1-934961-06-3

———————————————

Printed in the United States of America.

"Why does anybody tell a story?" Ms. L'Engle
*once asked, even though she knew the
answer. "It does indeed have something to do
with faith,"* she said, *"faith that the universe
has meaning, that human lives are not
irrelevant, that what we choose or say or do
matters, matters cosmically."*

Obituary for Madeleine L'Engle
New York Times
8 September 2007

To Joy Hoerner Rich,
who introduced me
to the Haders
and enriched my life.

TABLE OF CONTENTS

ILLUSTRATION & CAMEO CREDITS

Cover — Photographer unknown. (University of Oregon Collection).

Cover flap — Dedicatory watercolor in a copy of *Mr. Billy's Gun* (private collection of Joy Hoerner Rich)

Opposite Title — Berta: *Miss B.H.* by Elmer (1917)
Elmer: Self Portrait (1913)

Forward — Two Is Company, Three's a Crowd (Macmillan, 1965)

Preface — *Squirrelly of Willow Hill* (Macmillan, 1950)

Introduction — *Lost in the Zoo* (Macmillan, 1951)

Chapter 1 — *Billy Butter* (Macmillan, 1936)

Chapter 2 — *Mister Billy's Gun* (Macmillan, 1960)

Chapter 3 — *Midget and Bridget* (Macmillan, 1934)

Chapter 4 — *The Little Stone House* (Macmillan, 1944)

Chapter 5 — *Haders' Christmas Card* (1927)

Chapter 6 — *Working Together, The Inside Story of the Hader Books* (Macmillan, 1937)

Chapter 7 — *Jamaica Johnny* (Macmillan, 1935)

Chapter 8 — *Little White Foot* (Macmillan, 1952)

Chapter 9 — *Snow in the City* (Macmillan, 1963)

Chapter 10 — *Little Town* (Macmillan, 1941)

Chapter 11 — *The Big Snow* (Simon & Schuster, 1967)

Chapter 12 — *Rainbow's End* (Macmillan, 1946)

Chapter 13 — *The Cat and the Kitten* (Macmillan, 1940)

Chapter 14 — *Quack Quack* (Macmillan, 1961)

Acknowledgments — *Ding Dong Bell* (Macmillan, 1957)

FOREWORD

Drawn Together opens with an accident. A workman renovating a run-down stone house in Nyack, New York, falls through the roof into a secret room filled with drawings, paintings, manuscripts, and letters from a golden age of children's book illustration.

Sybilla Cook's biography of Berta and Elmer Hader, two outstanding artists of that period, is in itself a gateway into that almost forgotten era when American children's book publishing began. In page after page we run into the artists, editors, publishers, and writers who created the genre: Frederic Melcher, the Petershams, Rose Wilder Lane, Willy Pogany, Louise Seaman, Anne Carroll Moore. We are there at the beginning and, regrettably, at the end, when legal decisions and profound changes in the nature of the book publishing business brought that era to a close. The repercussions remain with us today.

Sybilla Cook has written an important book that deserves a prominent place among scholarly studies of children's literature.

ERIC KIMMEL

PREFACE

Berta and Elmer Hader's books were part of my growing up years, and they were still on the bookshelves when I became a librarian. Their Caldecott Award stickers indicated they were outstanding artists, and the animal stories were appealing, but I hadn't thought much about the people behind the books. When the University of Oregon sent an exhibit of picture book art to the local Douglas County Museum in Roseburg, Oregon, I was amazed. The Hader art pieces, mounted as individual pictures instead of as part of a book, really stood out among other illustrations.

When I found out I knew their niece in Roseburg, Joy Hoerner Rich, I began asking questions about what her aunt and uncle were like. Every time we talked, new interesting facts were revealed. Many of their journalist, writer, and artist friends made when they were young and starting out in San Francisco were now names I knew—such as Dorothy Parker, Will Irwin, Katherine Anne Porter, and Rose Wilder Lane. Another fact was that they now not only kept these friends after moving to New York City after World War I, but also added new friends and held an open house for them every weekend. Mary Margaret McBride, the Oprah of the 1930s, once said, "When I tell people about the Haders, they think they're a figment of my imagination." Laura Ingalls Wilder's daughter, Rose Wilder Lane, was homesick in Paris when she said that Berta and Elmer were the only people she knew who were already leading successful lives.

They'd built their own house on an "unbuildable" lot with the help of all these opinionated and artistic friends. Everyone helped cut brush, move heavy brownstones and lay the house foundation. Though they had different backgrounds and occupations, they got along well under the influence of Elmer's enthusiasm and warm hospitality and Berta's serene spirit and fine cooking.

That spirit of accommodation and cooperation had impressed Maine Senator Olympia Snowe when she visited a Falmouth map store in August 2010 to purchase a reproduction of the Hader's 1932 picture book map of Maine. It shows the couple, along with an explorer, a Native American, and an early Québécois, looking approvingly at Maine's diverse group of lumberjacks, potato farmers, lobstermen, skiers, paddlers, hikers, farmers, golfers, and college students going about their daily lives in a cooperative and peaceful manner. Snowe told the shop's owner, John Barrows, she'd recently been in a Washington discussion about bi-partisanship. To make her point about getting along, the first thing she thought of was that Hader map of her diverse state.

Besides being artists, writers, and builders, the Haders had also taken on the powers that be in New York State to save their own little town—Grand View-on-Hudson—from being torn down to make way for the Tappan Zee Bridge. How did they do that? It was another puzzle piece to discover.

By the time Joy suggested that she would like to see a biography of her Hader aunt and uncle, it sounded like a fun project about fascinating people. However, when I approached some professional book agents about the possibility of a biography, they were uniformly discouraging. Couldn't I find a few examples of dysfunction? Problems? No one would want to read about a happy marriage!

Of course they had problems. The Haders were real people who lived through family losses, the San Francisco earthquake, the Great Depression, and two major and some minor wars. They were constantly short of money in their early days, and reworked their art careers often as the market and outside world changed around them. Yet none of their many surviving letters complain about problems—except for the constant winter grouse about shoveling their long steep driveway over and over again! They had not thought of New York snowfalls when they built their house.

Their story seemed real to me, and I knew I would like to read about people who might have been my friends if years and space had not intervened. Berta and Elmer were—and are—examples of charm and resilience. *Drawn Together* incorporates many anecdotes from their own writings and those of their friends to illustrate how the Haders developed this happy marriage and productive life.

They were functional citizens in every sense of the word.

SYBILLA AVERY COOK

THE HIDDEN ROOM

Who were Berta and Elmer Hader?

When their niece, Joy Hoerner Rich, first suggested a Hader biography, I was hesitant—and curious. After inheriting some of the family-owned letters, books, and artwork, Joy had founded a non-profit group, Hader Connection, Ltd., to display and share examples of all the genres of Hader art: oil landscapes and portraits, paper activity toys for children, tiny portraits on ivory, cover art for *Metropolitan* magazine, book jackets and bookplates, art deco illustrations for books and stories, maps, and sketches. Joy asked Karen Tolley, owner of an antique book business and restorer of old books, about a possible biography. Karen thought it a great idea and suggested me as a possible writer.

As a former children's librarian I knew and admired the works of these Caldecott winning picture book artist/authors, but knew little about them as people. Who were they really, outside of their outstanding work in the picture book field? Was there enough substance for an adult biography?

To find out, I wanted to see where they'd lived. Because they'd lived all their married lives in a self-built home in Nyack, New York, entertained many of their outstanding artistic friends there, and frequently used this fairytale-like house as a book setting, this seemed to be where I could get a sense of place and a feel for their environment. Karen had written and called various people for permission to visit. Even though no one had responded, the three of us decided we could research Berta and Elmer even if we couldn't visit Willow Hill. So we flew off from our Oregon homes to the tiny village of Grand View-on-Hudson.

Joy had grown up in Oregon with many memories of her aunt and uncle. They kept in touch by mail. Joy recalls,

> "Every Christmas we children would wait for our parents to open the Haders' poster sized Christmas card. It always showed them as characters, in the clothing and setting of their forthcoming book, which we knew would be waiting for us under the Christmas tree. They might be riding an elephant (*Little Elephant,* 1930) or dressed in Dutch clothing and feeding goats in a barnyard with a rooster singing on a fence (*Cock-a-Doodle-Doo: Story of a Little Red Rooster,* 1939) or digging through massive piles of snow while small rabbits and skunks watch hopefully (*The Big Snow,* 1948). Each gift book would have a special hand drawn and personal dedication for the recipient, making the Haders always part of the family."

Though Joy hadn't been back to the Haders' "Little Stone House" for many years, she remembered some of the famous weekends in the forties when friends and editors such as Mary Margaret McBride, Bessie Beatty, Dorothy Parker, and Rose Wilder Lane, among others, would share personal memories and opinions of Russia, India or other exotic places.

Neither Karen nor I had ever seen it. Although we'd heard (wrongly) that a New York developer had torn down the house, we hoped wandering the grounds would give us a sense of the Haders' personalities. They had been able to buy the lot only because the abandoned brownstone quarry was considered unbuildable. Both had hauled rocks and cleared brush in order to build a beautiful home over a waterfall. Their house became a magnet for many of New York City's creative people. The property, preserved in as natural a state as possible, was home to a vast assortment of wildlife.

We three settled in a Nyack motel room, planning to visit the library and museum the next day. But in the morning we received a call from the present owner of the Hader property, Mark Goldstein. He had just received Karen's letter. Far from the stereotype of an uncaring developer, he was a charming man who'd grown up in the area. As a youngster he had often ridden his bike past the property along River Road, and wondered about the people who lived in the house on the hill with a waterfall spilling out from underneath. When he could finally afford to purchase it, he found a building with crumbling mortar that had become seriously deteriorated after passing through several owners. But he hadn't torn the house down—he'd done a major restoration. He saved the beautiful front stone façade with its magical view of the Hudson, the garden walls and stonework, the waterfall, and as many of Berta's beloved trees as possible.

What's more, he told Joy, he'd been hoping to hear from someone in the family.[1] While restoring the property, a worker had fallen
through the roof into the attic. He landed in a small dry-walled room,
with no door or any other means of egress. Neither of the previous
owners—old or young—had ever found it. It was packed full of art—
old pictures, linoleum blocks, and rolls of paper. Instead of thinking
it just old stuff and tossing it into the nearby dumpster, Mr. Goldstein
saved it because he knew who the Haders had been. He carefully set
the materials aside in a dry unlit room underneath the studio, hoping
a relative would show up to retrieve it. And he would be delighted to
have us come to the house and see it inside and out.

Excited, we drove up the long, steep driveway: the one that
the Haders had spent much of the winter shoveling by hand. (It
now had an automatic snow-melting system —Elmer would have
loved it.) Mark and son Daniel welcomed us into their remodeled
house: Joy found it looked much as she had last seen it. The new
flooring had been specially milled to match the original chestnut
boards, and the studio with its tall north windows was now a library. Designed after Elmer's studio in France, it was elevated a
few steps above the living room. Here Berta and Elmer had their
desks and easels and had worked together on book illustrations.
On weekends it turned into an impromptu stage with friends writing scripts and acting them out. Writer Katherine Anne Porter had
thoroughly enjoyed indulging her thespian talents there.

A small corner stairway still led from the studio to the Haders'
bedroom with its wonderful view of the Hudson and the Tappan
Zee Bridge with its unusual bend to the north. The guest bedrooms remained in a separate area; these were where Berta and
Elmer occasionally housed rescued animals. Guests often shared

their rooms with "Squirrely" or "Freddy the Phoebe." The grounds outside still had their small ponds and gardens, the old pignut tree, and the magical waterfall spilling from underneath the house. Terraces on all sides provided shady or sunlit spots, depending on what was wanted. It was easy to picture Berta and Elmer working in the gardens, reading on the patio, or putting seed into one of nineteen birdhouses they had built into the house walls.

Then we descended an original brick pathway past some ponds and entered a small dry room tucked under the studio. Here was the secret stash, now piled high on wooden shelves. Imagine having this treasure come to life after being hidden away for so long! Obviously the biography was meant to be written.

When the seven cartons of art arrived at Joy's home some time later, rewrapped and boxed in archival paper, each item was as immaculate as when it had been put away. The vivid colors seemed to have been freshly painted. The detailed black and white drawings were exquisite. It was a hugely varied collection.

Obviously, much of the work had been done when Berta and Elmer were artists struggling to make a living. The different types of artwork showed attempts to reach every possible art market. There were jackets for pulp novels, romantic pictures with stylized knights and maidens, proofs for picture books, individual book plate designs, a variety of sketches, linoleum blocks for their annual poster sized Christmas cards, pen and ink drawings that looked like etchings, magazine covers, and more of the hands-on cutout toys that had been such popular additions to the magazines of the 1920s. The collection, lovingly preserved and long forgotten, added a new dimension to the Hader exhibits. These previously unseen pieces showed not only their versatility, but also the different styles and particular preferences throughout the twentieth century.

These were artists who would have been outstanding in any field of art they chose. Fortunately, they chose the field of children's books, where they have influenced and inspired generations of children. Recently, an architect in Eugene, Oregon, entered the framing shop where some of these newly-discovered paintings were being mounted for an exhibit. He instantly recognized the style as the Haders and told the owner that their book about the building of "The Little Stone House" had inspired his career choice.

Berta and Elmer would have been pleased and proud.

CHAPTER ONE

TELEGRAPH HILL: ARTS AND HEARTS

TELEGRAPH

As I went up to Telegraph
Up rough and rugged Telegraph,
The day was fair on Telegraph;
The air was gold with sun.
Along the slanting, cobbled street
The children played on agile feet
Their laughter chimed so clear and sweet
I loved them every one.

And then I stood on Telegraph
And looked away from Telegraph.
And, oh, the bay from Telegraph,
As bright as polished steel!
The bay that sparkles blue at noon
The bay that's never out of tune
With any mood I feel!

– Dmitri Bary[2]

$\mathcal{T}$elegraph Hill at 274 feet was the highest point seen when sailing through the golden gate passage into San Francisco Bay. The semaphore tower located on top with flags on arms like the messenger flags used aboard ships telegraphed the approach of clipper ships. "When the signal went up that a ship was coming in, the crowds started running and by the time she arrived at Long's Wharf, a clamoring mob would be yelling for mail, election returns from the East, or goods to buy."[3]

The hill was originally settled by Irish immigrants and a smattering of Germans, and later by the Italian dockworkers. They sent home for their families and the North Beach area became known as Little Italy.[4] The hill was extremely steep. Many visitors were kept away by the periodic noise and shaking from the stone quarry that provided ballast for the ships in the harbor. The stones also provided ammunition for the local children who had a reputation for bullying outsiders. Like many other San Franciscans, Elmer and his brothers had avoided the area.

But now, as an artist newly returned from Paris, he had accepted a challenge to paint this community that had survived the 1906 San Francisco Earthquake and subsequent fires. Elmer had been gone from the city for several years, first traveling across the United States with a vaudeville show and then studying art in Paris. The imminence of the Great War had sent him and others back to their home countries, and Elmer had returned to his parents' home in San Francisco's Mission District in time for the Panama-Pacific International Exposition of 1915. The city was eager to show how it had revitalized itself only nine years after the quake. This exhibition showcasing all types of fine art from various countries brought many visitors to the area, including young artists and journalists from all over the United States. It intensified Elmer's conviction that he could become a leading San Francisco Impressionist. He built himself an art studio in his parents' attic and set out to paint scenes around the bay.

As he trudged up Telegraph Hill one day, Elmer realized why his artist friend suggested he go there to paint the houses above the harbor area. Not only would the view from the top be spectacular, but the old cottages with their "irresponsible architecture"[5] had a certain charm. He realized that even though he had spent most of his twenty-six years in San Francisco, he had never explored Telegraph Hill.

Elmer dreaded lugging his paraphernalia up and down the rugged hill. But the friend said she knew an artist/journalist who might be willing to store his heavy paint boxes in her little studio at the top of the hill. It was one of three artist studios built by poet Harry Lafler[6] from the construction remnants of the giant redwood WELCOME sign that had been erected in 1908. The 50-foot-high letters were visible for thirty miles and easily seen from Theodore Roosevelt's "Great White Fleet" as it came to California on its way to circumnavigate the world.

Now it was time to meet the artist and see if she'd store his paraphernalia. Elmer left the Kearney Street streetcar at Broadway and climbed up a long block of steps to Vallejo Street. The vibrant neighborhood reminded him of being on Montmartre, with its struggling artists and immigrants chattering in a mélange of languages. As he trudged up the hill, he realized his friend was right—these "ramshackle houses clinging like swallows' nests under the eaves" were picturesque and would be interesting to paint. The 1906 fires had destroyed many of the original residences on the hill, but those in the Italian area had survived: their occupants had covered the roofs with blankets doused in barrels of home-made wine.

He turned on Union and trudged up to the "ragged, rugged end of Montgomery Street with its dejected pretension at side-walks."[7] He was surrounded by urchins talking in a conglomeration of Italian, Spanish, and broken English. He passed Filbert, known as the Street of a Thousand Stairs and entered the "yellow footpath" of Montgomery Street, as it zigzagged upward on a green slope where Spanish children herded goats.[8] He couldn't help but be re-minded of a verse by former San Francisco journalist Wallace Irwin.

> The Irish they live on the top av it,
> And th' Dagoes they live on th' base av it,
> And th' goats and th' chicks
> And th' brickbats and shticks
> Is joombled all over th' face av it!
> On Telygraft Hill, Telygraft Hill,
> Crazy owld, daisy owld, Telygraft Hill![9]

Finally reaching the crest, he found the studios were charm-ing, set among the broken-down stone walls and eucalyptus trees of a former park.[10] From here he could see the city's busy harbor, the Piedmont Hills behind Oakland, and Mount Tamalpais to the north.[11] He looked forward to meeting the woman who must man-age walking up and down this hill every day.

Berta Hoerner turned out to be delightful. Tall and willowy with a mop of untamable curls, she had an infectious smile. She welcomed this dashing young impressionist with his reddish locks and European air. She was sympathetic to his ambitions and un-derstood why he desired to paint these unlovely shacks with the gorgeous views. They drank tea, listened to violinist Fritz Kreisler on the phonograph, and talked art. They had much in common, since Berta was taking classes at the California School of Design— his alma mater. Her specialty was miniature portraits: full color portraits of children painted on thin slices of ivory the size of business cards. It was a completely opposite field from his sweeping landscape painting. By the time he left, she'd not only agreed to store his painting supplies but also told him where the key was hidden, so he could pick them up while she was at work.

Berta said she loved living in a house made out of a welcome sign,[12] and she certainly was welcoming to everyone she met. The more he saw of Berta, the more he found himself enchanted by this woman who was the center of a large group of friends. He showed up to paint Telegraph Hill nearly every day, arriving around ten in the morning. He painted the shacks from every possible angle and was often persuaded to stay on for an evening get together with Berta's close friends, many of them writers and journalists living nearby.

One of these was Bessie Beatty[13], head of the Women's Page for the *San Francisco Bulletin.* Berta had met her soon after taking over Eva Shepherd's fashion illustration business. Bessie liked Berta's artwork and later asked Berta to illustrate some of writer Rose Wilder Lane's feature page stories, including Lane's "The People in Our Apartment House." Berta had already found Rose to be "a gay and charming companion" who had lived with husband Gillette Lane in the same Russian Hill building as she did. Others in the Lombard Street building were Sara Field Bard, suffragist and poet, and Oregon attorney and artist Charles Erskine Scott Wood. They had left Oregon together and were waiting for divorces from their respective spouses. When the Bard/Woods moved out of their apartment, Sara's sister Mary Field

Parton moved in with her husband Lem, also a journalist for the *San Francisco Bulletin.* Berta sometimes looked after their little daughter, Margaret. Rose's mother, Laura Ingalls Wilder, mentioned the "little artist girl in the basement" when she wrote to husband Manly about her visit to Rose during the 1915 Panama–Pacific International Exposition.[14]

By the time Berta decided to move to the brown-shingled studio at 1413 Montgomery Street, she, Bessie, and Rose were fast friends. Rose's marriage was beginning to unravel, and she decided to rent the studio next door to Berta. Laura wrote to Manly, "The places are rather dilapidated but can be fixed very cozily." The gorgeous views made up for the fact that it was in a rundown working class area. Laura was relieved when Rose changed her mind about moving: "the landlady who lives next door with seven children, gets drunk and fights."[15] Later, Rose changed her mind again, left Gillette, and moved to Telegraph Hill.

Laura's qualms aside, Berta never felt threatened by their neighbors. They were kind and gracious family people, with adorable children who often posed for Berta's miniature portraits. However, one night Berta came home after dark and found the place surrounded by police: apparently drug addicts were hiding in the neighborhood.[16]

Elmer was extremely upset. He spoke to one of his police friends, who advised him that addicts often hung around the area, and offered to have a policeman escort Berta home. Elmer said no, he would take over the escort job himself—a good excuse to see more of this interesting woman.

Berta had a gift for friendship and was always surrounded by old and new friends. Her temporary roommates included Bessie and Paula Cunningham, a nurse friend from Seattle, whose older sister Imogen was becoming a well-known photographer. The friends who clustered around the studios were an eclectic group of passionate people Elmer thought were "extremely talky." At first he was overwhelmed by the seemingly brilliant conversation: the newspaper people and writers constantly talked over, around, and through each other.

Writer Freddy O'Brien, recently returned from the Marquesa Islands in the South Seas, was the "greatest storyteller who ever lived." Stella Karn was a circus publicist, small and noisy, with "a mouth like a half-moon." One of her favorite stories on herself was about taking the baby circus elephant out on walks: "from the rear you couldn't tell which was Stella and which was the elephant."

Poet Dmitri Bary was a lively center of attention with a "lion dance" he performed on Berta's couch and a talent for making and fixing things. (On a return some ten years later, Rose was delighted to find a table he had had made for her was still being used, though the new renters had no idea it was hinged so it could drop down out of the way.) The lion dance on the sofa became one of the legends related about Telegraph Hill's early days.[17] A Swiss musician, Jean-Jacques Marquis, also joined the group.

Artist Ernest Haskell had also attended the Académie Julian in Paris, though a decade before Elmer. Guy Moyston was a feature article writer for the Associated Press, while Lem Parton, former gold miner, cowboy, and explorer, was currently writing for the *Bulletin.* A big-hearted and genial man, he was always welcome at any gathering. His wife, Mary Parton, was a magazine writer and passionate supporter of the underdog. She had once lived and worked with Jane Addams at Hull House, the famous settlement house in Chicago.

Elmer's self-confidence, honed from years in vaudeville, easily made him a part of this "talky group," as did his artistic studies abroad. He had a great sense of humor, and quickly became a part of Berta's crowd, along with his musician and artist friends from the Bohemian Club.[18] Twenty or more might cram into the tiny studio quarters, eating Berta's famous "gypsy stew" or fresh bread and cheeses from the Italian markets at the bottom of the hill.

Elmer and Berta enjoyed this lively crowd of divergent personalities. They gradually found they had much in common besides their art, even though their personalities were different. Elmer was usually the center of attention, while Berta was self-effacing. Even though five foot seven, she was often described as "little." She described herself once as "timid but I knew what I wanted to do." He was impetuous and full of ideas: she was quietly determined and usually figured out how to get what she wanted. Both came from caring families but knew it was up to them to make their own futures. The more they talked, took long walks around the city admiring the mysteriousness of Chinatown and the bustling business center, admired new buildings and gorgeous gardens, the more they found similarities in their different upbringings. Each had loved to sketch at a young age, and both had been recognized early as having artistic talent. Each had had third grade teachers who allowed them to draw on the blackboards in colored chalk. Both had been good at handmade crafts; in sixth grade Elmer had even constructed his own banjo from scratch, decorating it with inlays cut from pearl collar buttons. He'd also learned to play the piano by ear, making him a hit at parties.

Berta must have been fascinated when Elmer, blue eyes twinkling behind his spectacles, regaled her with stories about his past. Some sounded too amazing to be true. His mother, Lena Nyberg, had arrived from Sweden as a child and later married Henry Hader, a former Civil War soldier from Pennsylvania. Henry worked on the railroads as they crossed the United States, and they followed his work across the country until finally ending in San Francisco. Henry continued his railroad work there on the San Francisco Belt Line—a short line connecting the piers with the city, meaning he could be home every night.

Elmer was born in Pajaro, California,[19] on 7 September 1889, but lived in San Francisco from his first birthday on. As a little boy he spent time on a nearby ranch and wanted to raise horses when he grew up. A sketch of a boy feeding a colt, drawn when Elmer was only seven, followed them to their house in Grand View-on-Hudson.[20]

He expected to go to the California School of Design of the Mark Hopkins Institute of Art when he finished high school, but his plans "went up in smoke" when the 1906 San Francisco earthquake—the most destructive earthquake in American history—hit the city. As a sixteen-year-old bugler with the Coast Artillery of the National Guard, he was called to service. "The first few days of the fire, our fire company was in the heart of the city, saving supplies," he recalled. "We dashed in and out of the burning buildings carrying armfuls of groceries as the firemen played the water hoses above our heads. The heavy smoke so filled the air we couldn't tell if it was night or day."[21] In spite of all valiant efforts, the fire burned out of control for three days destroying some 28,000 buildings. Elmer's parents lost all they owned, including the potato yeast used as a starter for Lena's homemade bread.

Since an immigrant woman who'd brought it with her from Ireland had given it to Lena, it could never be replicated. Elmer always remembered missing that bread.[22]

Elmer apprenticed as a silversmith, worked as a stock clerk in a hardware store and then found a job with a surveying party near Sacramento. After the surveying job ended, he found a new job firing locomotives for the San Francisco Belt Line. When he wasn't called on to fire locomotives, he swept the floor and polished the brass and found the nights long and monotonous.[23] When the California School of Design reopened in 1907. Elmer used his savings to enroll. From then on, he earned a tuition free scholarship every year.

Like Elmer, Berta also studied at the California School of Design, so they had much to share. She'd led a peripatetic childhood since her 1 August 1890 birth in San Pedro, Mexico. As a young girl, her mother, Adelaide Jennings, had lived in southern Texas on a ranch 45 miles from Uvalde, Texas, where she "loved beyond anything else the freedom to explore alone and on horseback . . . what was such a strange country, with mountains shaped like pyramids . . . rocky, barren land but for cactus . . . where old trails of Indians wound throughout the hills." She remembered one of old General Baylor's sons calling her a mad Yankee because she didn't mind that it was hot. Adelaide wrote, "I explored the mountains carrying a little bottle of lime juice with me to quench my thirst, and then writing a note and corking it inside and hiding the bottle in a crevice for some future climber to find."[24]

Since her businessman father, William Jennings, had taken his family with him as he traveled all over the United States, Adelaide grew up wanting to stay in one place. She decided to marry a German because "they never move. I will have a stone bench at my back door and I will wear a groove in it sitting there."[25] But Albert Hoerner, German though he was, moved to Mexico where he joined his brother in a cotton-growing enterprise. Adelaide, once married, faced a "life behind mud walls and iron bars . . . the seclusion and lack of freedom was not at all to my liking." She dressed Berta "as nearly minus" as possible at a time when babies were bundled up and tried to ensure that "Berta could grow freely."[26]

Adelaide's mother had been an oil painter, and Adelaide herself spent much of her time behind those mud walls making watercolor sketches of picturesque Mexicans, quaint houses, and courtyards. Berta must have been fascinated watching her mother make pictures out of everyday life and undoubtedly sketched right along with her mother. Adelaide always encouraged her art.

The brothers' cotton business proved unsuccessful. When Berta was only three, the Hoerners moved again: first to Parras, Mexico, and then to Amarillo, Texas, where Albert managed a small grocery store. Adelaide added to the family income by running a kindergarten while caring for Berta and her newborn brother Godfrey.[27] Albert knew of his wife's desire for a piece of land, so he gave her some land on a hilltop for her birthday. But on "the last day of August [her] husband was dead."[28] He died of consumption, only two years after the move to Texas.

Adelaide, determined to support her children by herself, moved to Kansas City to be a social worker. Berta was in third grade there when she won an essay contest and received "a very fine copy of Tom Sawyer."[29] This inspired her to think of a career in writing, even though her mother thought Berta should keep on developing her artistic skills.

Elmer's mother had also encouraged her son's interest in art. She insisted the double crown of hair he had at birth predestined him to be an artist.[30] She was not surprised when he won scholarships, including one granting him free tuition at the Académie Julian in Paris, an eclectic school with teachers who were both liked and admired. The academy encouraged new ideas and had a long history of distinguished and international alumni such as Henri Matisse, Marcel DuChamp, Emily Carr, and Edward Steichen.[31]

A French education was considered mandatory for any American artist who hoped to be taken seriously. However, Elmer would have to pay for his travel to Paris and would also have to plan for several years of room and board. He knew his family couldn't afford to send him. He and Edward Holl, friend and fellow Julian scholarship winner, decided they could make good money by forming a vaudeville act.[32] Both had learned to be unmoving models for senior classes at art school, so they formed an act called "Visions in Marble" representing the "rosy dreams of a discouraged artist." They posed as classic Greek statues such as "The Discus Thrower." A Colorado Springs paper said, "Their work is so flawless that as the lights play upon them in their classic postures they seem as if carved of pure white marble." The effect was produced by "good lighting, tights or similar clothing, drapes," and occasionally plaster of Paris, white chalk, gilt, or talc. To attract more attention and thus make more money, they added two young women to the show. "The youths were handsome, the poses striking, and audiences were appreciative." They secured a spot on the vaudeville circuit and toured the United States. All was going well until one awful night when they were unable to remove the plaster from their models. "Stiff-faced, the frightened 'statues' could not speak, but tears oozed from their eyes and rolled down their white coating." When Elmer finally succeeded in removing the mixture, the girls refused to talk to him or Edward. As he said, when later recounting this story, "there was "dissension in the troops."[33]

Elmer was known for telling a good story, and this one must have impressed his listeners.

Berta's journey to art school was far less impressive. Her mother had a difficult time earning enough as a social worker to support the family, so they moved from Kansas City to her stockbroker father's home in Suffern, New York. Berta and younger brother Godfrey enrolled in the Suffern elementary schools. During summer vacation, her mother sent Berta to study drawing at an artist's studio, and apparently she achieved some success. Berta remembered being around age nine when "a friend of my mother's . . . ordered art work from me. I remember making a book of Sunbonnet Babies for her." The same friend also paid Berta for making place cards for her, and she was delighted to earn real money from her art.

Adelaide found a job in New York City and enrolled both children in the School of Ethical Culture so the family could commute together. [34] Later she moved her little family to Cleveland, where Berta graduated from high school in 1909. Adelaide then moved to Seattle where she had a job at the Washington Home and at the Charity Organization Society and where she married landscaper William Gordon. At last she had a garden with as many flowers as she wanted. In the author biography section of a poetry magazine that published one of Adelaide's poems, she is referred to as "a poet, a gardener and great humanist . . . [who] combines her three gifts by gathering bouquets, stowing them in a basket, goes downtown from Magnolia Hill, and gives them to people who look tired and unhappy." When Adelaide was a little girl she had often watched her father, William Jennings, go off to work with a basket of flowers on his arm, and at night she would hear him throw open his window and tell the world goodnight. "God bless the world," he would call into the dark.

Berta and her new stepfather, Billy Gordon, got along famously. He thoroughly enjoyed having young people in the house and called her "Fluffy," referring to her hair. He also enjoyed writing and encouraged her plans to study journalism and art.

Elmer, meanwhile, was still working on getting to France.[35] The demise of "Visions" was a setback, but Hader and Holl formed a less-expensive act by themselves. In "A Sketch A Minute," they would draw any subject proposed by the audience. This also proved to be popular and they received an offer for a ten-week tour in New York State.

Just as they were ready to start, Elmer's brother Waldo sent him a telegram. "Elmer, we have held family council. Decided no use continuing vaudeville. Do not book any more. Making plans for you for Paris. Don't delay to argue. Are making plans here."[36] A later letter from his father explained the arrangement. The family felt Elmer had wasted enough time. Brother Waldo was working in a meat market, so was able to send Elmer $10. Siblings Carl and Leota also chipped in.

> Now we want you to get ready to cross over without any further delay. Waldo will send you $100 or we will, anyway it will be Waldo's money, & we think that sufficient to take you over and locate you for a month. We will put in $10,

Waldo $10, Leota $5, and Carl $5. So you see it will not come down hard on any of us, & we all are willing and eager to assist you. So now don't try to give any back talk on this matter. Our minds are made up to this arrangement for your benefit, and see to it that you profit by your opportunity.[37]

Elmer and Edward dawdled long enough to finish the New York tour. By this time they rather liked stage life. After the two arrived in Paris they rented an attic studio on Impasse Marie Blanche and decided to earn some extra cash by doing a little acting on the side. They developed an act, "An Atelier Oddity," got a tryout at the Alhambra, and received a smashing response from the audience. Surprised when they heard nothing from the manager, they finally looked him up, only to be scolded for not replying to his telegram. He had been prepared to offer them "an excellent contract for several months" but it was all finished now—he would not deal with someone who lacked the courtesy to respond. Even when Elmer found and proved he had never received the missing wires, the manager refused to hire them. It was time to concentrate on art.

Once Holl and Hader actually started their studies at the Académie Julian, Elmer was surprised by the competence of the other artists. He had always been considered an outstanding art student, even at the California School of Design and assumed he would still be outstanding in Paris. It was a shock to find that in Paris he was only one of many good artists.[38] Not content to be just one of the many, he settled down to his studies under the direction of noted Impressionists François Flameng, Albert Deschenard, and Adolphe Duchaud. He took classes in illustration, figure, portrait, and "en plein air" landscape painting. Students were taught how to use the looser brushstroke favored by the impressionists and a "subdued and low-keyed palette."[39]

They were also taught the "Chevreul's Law of Simultaneous Contrast of Colors." It states, in part, "The apparent intensity of color does not depend as much on the inherent pigmentation . . . as it does on the hue of the neighboring color." Furthermore, Chevreul adds, "When two colored objects are scrutinized together, the color of each will be influenced by the complementary color of its neighbor."[40] These studies proved to be invaluable later, when Elmer had to work with the very limited palette offered by American printers.

Paris was alive with "colormen" selling a wide variety of synthetic and natural paints in the collapsible tin tubes developed half a century before. These offered the freedom to paint "en plein air," and the colormen could provide any hue an artist might need or want. These "portable paintboxes" were important to Impressionists. They could paint landscapes changing in differing lights—a movement perfect for a Californian in love with his native outdoor city. Elmer delighted in using them while he painted outdoors one summer in Brittany.

The two roommates shared one large gilded frame to display their paintings, so had to size them to fit. Elmer used the frame for a winter landscape he'd seen when touring in New York State. "Winter—Little Falls" was selected for the 1914 annual Salon Exhibit of the Societé des Artistes Français—an honor that might have led to more opportunities except for the imminence of the Great War. All expatriates had to leave Europe. Elmer stopped off in London to paint for a few months[41] before returning to the family's new home in the Mission District of San Francisco. He remodeled the upstairs into a studio, and set about becoming the premier California Impressionist.

After moving to Seattle, Berta was dismayed to discover there were no art schools anywhere. A friend told her the best way to learn art was from the staff artists at a printing company, who could teach her the basics. With her usual determination, Berta set out to get a job at one of them. She was turned down everywhere she applied. However, the manager at *Western Engraving and Colortype* must have seen something in the "young girl with tied back curls"[42] and said they might be hiring in the fall. With her usual persistence she returned in the fall. The manager must have been surprised but he hired her as a half-day apprentice at no pay. One of the company's advertising slogans was "Illustration Beats Explanation," and they hired many artists to prove it. It would be art training of a sort, and she could live at home and take journalism classes half days at the University of Washington.

The manager gave her a table and chair by a window in the storeroom and taught her how to enlarge pictures of household furnishings using a pantograph. It was boring work almost anybody could do, but she got to know many of the commercial artists who worked on staff, especially Eva Shepherd, one of the managers. After a year, she was offered a salary of three dollars a week, and then later a full-time job. That meant leaving the University of Washington,[43] but she was learning from Eva and the other artists.

Eva recognized Berta's artistic talent and taught her how to do fashion illustration. Berta's nearsightedness helped her see and draw the smallest details on the dresses of the day. Fashion was far more interesting than refrigerators and stoves. This attention to detail also led Eva to arrange for her sister Clare Shepherd, who painted miniature portraits on ivory, to give Berta lessons in that field. Berta loved it. One of Clare's friends was Imogen Cunningham, a photographer who had a studio nearby. They became lifelong friends, and Imogen photographed the Haders whenever she came to New York.

Eva had a side business as a freelance fashion designer and illustrator for the Seattle department stores of Frederick & Nelson and the Bon Marché. When Eva took a better job in San Francisco, she asked Berta to take over the Seattle assignments. In 1915, Eva moved again, this time to New York and offered Berta the chance to take over her California business. San Francisco had a number of good art schools, and she could further her art studies and still hold a paying job.

She accepted, left her mother and stepfather William Gordon and sailed to California. She knew two artists at the Chase School of Art in Carmel[44] and used some savings to take classes there that summer.[45] She took additional courses at the California School of Design while running Eva's business. Her free time was spent on art studies and on developing her abilities in miniature portraiture. These were watercolor paintings on one to three inch pieces of ivory, about the size of large postage stamps.

San Francisco hosted the Panama-Pacific International Exhibition in 1915, displaying the finest modern art from around the world. People from all over visited the Exhibition and discovered the attractiveness of the rebuilt city. A later director of the Palace of Fine Arts said, "San Francisco is one of the six leading cities of the country in attendance at art shows" partly due to the

400,000 who attended this exhibition.[46] Art students like Berta crowded through the gates to see examples of popular art from other countries.

Rose Wilder Lane and other journalists wrote related and interesting stories for their journals and often interviewed the rising young artists. One story portrayed Elmer as a dashing young man-about-town who had built his own studio in the attic of the family's home. Here he created many paintings from sketches done in Paris and London. The San Francisco Art Association exhibited some of these, and others were exhibited at the Oakland Municipal Gallery.[47]

By the time Berta and Elmer met in 1916, they were both becoming known in their different fields. He was garnering publicity in the local papers and was a member of the Bohemian Club for artists and writers. Berta was taking art classes while supporting herself with illustration work for the *Bulletin,* running Eva's business, and selling her tiny ivory portraits. She charged $125 each for these painted miniatures, often worn as lockets or mounted in larger gilt frames. Mother Adelaide said this amount was far too high since Berta had "not yet arrived."

Both budding artists enjoyed music and spent many hours listening to the latest classical music on the radio, as well as trying out the latest dances such as the fox trot in impromptu get togethers. They also attended many other types of musical entertainment, including "dinner dansants." Elmer's Bohemian Club hosted some of these.

A corsage Elmer sent her for one of these events enclosed a poem Berta kept all her life. It was written to fit in the flowers' tiny envelope.

Let these flowers say for me
Just how happy I shall be,
Dear, tonight.
Thinking of your dancing feet
Tripping through the moments. Fleet
With delight.

Dancing feet and dancing eyes—
Parted lips where laughter lies.
Curls that tease—
Oh, my love will follow you
While you dance the bright hours through,
Wearing these.[48]

Neither Berta nor Elmer could see anything but bright hours in their future. They were in love and would live on Telegraph Hill forever. What could possibly get in their way?

CHAPTER TWO

GREENWICH VILLAGE: NEW PATHS

*T*he events in Europe seemed remote from California. There were as wide a variety of opinions within the Telegraph Hill group as there were in the United States. Many—though not all—of America's German immigrants, were pro-Germany. Many Irish immigrants opposed anything favoring Great Britain, and the largest part of the electorate opposed entering the war at all. Woodrow Wilson, considered the pro-peace candidate, won the election in November 1916. The following April the man whose campaign slogan was "He Kept Us Out of War" asked Congress to declare one and authorized a draft of young men in May of 1917.

By that spring Russia was also center stage. Germany's successful thrust into Russia was blamed on the failures of Czar Nicholas II, and he was forced to abdicate in March. Several groups in Russia—radical, moderate, and conservative—began maneuvering to gain power. *San Francisco Bulletin* editor Fremont Older, one of the forward-thinking editors of the day, gave Bessie Beatty an almost unheard-of assign-ment for a woman. She was to cover the Kerensky takeover of the Russian government as the paper's war correspondent.

Meanwhile, Elmer had rented a studio for himself near Berta, while he worked on preparing for his first one-man show of his Tele-graph Hill and Fisherman's Wharf paintings. This would be the first San Francisco show devoted to a single artist with a single theme— a real coup for a rising young star. The show opened on 28 Novem-ber 1917 with decidedly mixed reviews. Many San Franciscans did not appreciate his portrayal of those unlovely shacks and working docks, suggesting he should have concentrated on the city's lovely gardens and beaches. *San Francisco Examiner* critic Marie David-son described Hader as an "Exponent of the homely and common place of art." More modern critics appreciated his technique and "the strength of the paintings, the intimate knowledge and feel for the subject, his sincerity in painting his impressions of the area with freshness of vision and vitality so as to bring beauty and dignity to what others, less inspired, viewed as nothing but grim poverty and squalor."[49] Elmer, in an article in *The Wasp*, said he hoped his paintings would enable viewers to see beauty in what heretofore seemed ugliness."[50] Rose Wilder Lane's article in the *Bulletin* said that Elmer's paintings show Telegraph Hill's appeal "with its charm of quaintness" and "the underlying beauty and romance" of the Spanish workingmen's cottages and the always filled clotheslines.[51]

The controversy didn't hurt Elmer's reputation. Another prized exhibition was in the works. Three of his figural works would be exhibited in the San Francisco Art Association's Annual Exhibi-tion the following March. Among these would be Elmer's gift to his fiancée: his painting of Berta, *Portrait of Miss B.H.*[52] Berta would also be exhibiting her miniature portraits of the Telegraph Hill children in the same show.

Much as the couple tried to ignore it, the war began to spill over into their personal lives. Rose Wilder Lane had expected to get the Russian assignment. When it went to Bessie, Rose still stuck with local stories finding it hard to compete with Bessie's war dispatches on the front page. Artist Ernest Haskell was commissioned to help develop camouflage techniques. He and his colleagues were using their knowledge of color to paint objects so they would seem invisible from at least a mile away.[53]

Elmer was still dealing with controversial reviews when his draft notice arrived. He was to join the Camouflage Corps of the American Expeditionary Force, where his French skills and artistic abilities would be put to use. Luckily, his unit was to remain in San Francisco and train at the Presidio next to San Francisco Bay.

Berta's brother Godfrey also joined the army that fall. Her mother and stepfather William Gordon wanted the family to be together for a final Christmas before he went overseas. Berta was torn. She wished to spend every possible minute with Elmer, especially this particular Christmas. She and Elmer talked it over, and finally decided that this might be her last chance to see Godfrey for a long time, but Elmer would still be in San Francisco when she returned. She made plans for a two week trip. Once she arrived in Seattle, the family learned that Godfrey would not be there—the Army had other plans. She stayed on to keep her mother and stepfather company, but kept up a daily correspondence with Elmer. (His letters, illustrated with pencil sketches, kept telling her not to weep so much about his being gone, that he would be waiting anxiously for her arrival.) Berta treasured and kept his Christmas card and tender illustrated letters to his "curly top" all her life.[54]

Both looked forward to their upcoming exhibits at the Palace of Fine Arts. However, shortly after Berta returned from Seattle, Elmer's unit was ordered to New York to prepare for their overseas assignments. Although there was never a formal proposal of marriage, they knew they were meant to be together always. Berta decided to follow him to New York and be with him until he sailed.

Bessie Beatty had recently returned to New York City from Russia. She and other American journalists, including John Reed, Louise Bryant, and Ernestine Evans, had been covering the hostilities. Bessie had gone to the front lines where the "Battalion of Death" was fighting the Germans under the leadership of a peasant woman, Marie Bacharova. Appointed the first full-fledged female officer in the Russian army, she led her women's battalion to the front lines, where they fought in place of the army deserters.[55]

Bessie's courage, stamina, and reports impressed *McCall's Magazine* enough that she was hired to be their editor. Delighted when she heard Berta was coming to New York, she immediately offered Berta a chance to do the fashion illustrations in the magazine. She also invited Berta to stay with her until she could find something suitable to rent.

Berta immediately resigned from the *Bulletin*, gave up her studio, and packed all her possessions into a couple of tall Chinese baskets to take on the train.[56] By the time the Annual Exhibition took place, neither was there to accept their accolades. Berta's six miniatures were praised as "Unusually well done: they are not mere painting . . . [she] has caught much of the lovely Latin spirit of her subjects; she has gone under their skins." And Elmer's portrait of "Miss B.H." received praise as a "sensitively executed portrait of the fresh-faced and vital young woman." [57] The show's reviews were very good, and Berta's portrait graced the front page of the *San Francisco Bulletin* on 20 April.

Unfortunately, Berta's train was far slower than the one used by the American Expeditionary Force. While en route she received a terse telegram from friends in New York City who knew she was coming to see Elmer off to France. The text was ambiguous: "Elmer's gone." She hadn't expected a telegram and worried about its meaning. Did "gone" mean "expired"? Surely not. When she finally arrived she was relieved to find it meant only to tell her he had already sailed for France.[58]

New York City, considered by many to be the literary center of the United States, was an exciting place to be in 1918. Sparked by the large influx of college-educated women earlier in the decade, it was a community where, "for a brief time, art and politics, earnestness and good companionship mingled" and rents were cheap. It offered individual freedom, privacy, and communal events of intellectual appeal.[59] There were editorials and street demonstrations about everything: from corruption, economic justice, pacifism, anarchism, the Russian Revolution, birth control and women's suffrage, to the demise of the petticoat and the new fad of "close dancing."[60] Greenwich Village was "the intellectual and spiritual center of these movements. Supposedly anyone who climbed a soapbox there would have a crowd of followers in an hour."[61] Bessie and Berta gradually immersed themselves in this world, seeing old friends from California and making new ones.

A variety of artistic outlets were available. *The Masses* magazine began as a collective project where contributors and editors would gather and argue about other contributors' essays and poetry. Modern art hung in saloons as well as art galleries. The Provincetown Players, a group formed in Massachusetts to put on the new and/or modern plays that mainstream theaters ignored, had just branched out to the Washington Square area. (This group performed Eugene O'Neill's first play, *Bound East for Cardiff*.)[62]

Rose Wilder Lane arrived in New York on her way back to San Francisco. She'd resigned from the *Bulletin* earlier in 1918, when the paper's owners made it impossible for Fremont Older, the editor who had attracted the original group of eager and talented writers, to stay. Many left, including Rose who moved to Sausalito to help turn friend Frederick O'Brien's South Seas stories into a publishable book. She was soon offered a wartime publicity job with the Red Cross in Washington, D.C. Her job ended when the Armistice was signed and peace was declared, so she planned to return to California and finish the O'Brien manuscript.

Bessie, whose managerial efforts had won her the nickname of "Mother Beatty" in San Francisco, convinced Rose that New York was the only place for a vital, searching young woman to live, and she should stay in this "cultural center of the USA." However, Bessie, busily turning her war dispatches into a book, *The Red Heart of Russia*, didn't have room for another roommate. Rose and Berta, former Telegraph Hill neighbors, decided to team up and rent a rundown four-story house at 31 Jones Street.

There was no central heating, and it was December, but the girls from California didn't even realize that might be a problem. Their tin-ceilinged kitchen and dining room were in the English-style basement, four steps down from street level. Steep, narrow stairs led up to the living room on the first floor and the bedrooms and studio up more flights of stairs. As their California friends came through New York on their way to and from Europe or to work in the city, they found Telegraph Hill hospitality in the Jones Street house . . . for a day and sometimes longer until they could find living quarters of their own. One of these was writer Eve Chappel, who even Rose considered a very fine writer.[63]

Many years later Rose wrote about this Greenwich Village experience to her friend Dorothy Thompson.[64]

> Simultaneously Berta arrived to say goodbye to Elmer, her fiancé, who had been drafted: he was shipped before she arrived. She had no money, I had $100.00, so we leased an empty house on Jones Street . . . and were shocked when the landlord demanded $100.00 in advance, 2 month's rent, to guarantee the lease. We borrowed $25 from Bessie Beatty, and lived that winter on 50 cents a day; split pea soup, nothing else, and I still love split pea soup.
>
> We slept, heaven knows why, on a bedspring (which someone gave us) on the floor, under newspapers and all our clothes: and woke in the morning, deeply impressed like waffles, by the bedsprings. No heat. The place seemed infested by rats at night, but we soon discovered it was a ghost.
>
> We had a grand time and many delightful adventures. By day Berta worked at her drawing board and I at my typewriter, wearing all the clothes that could be superimposed and frequently warming our hands in our armpits. And I wrote the tender and touching story of the carrier pigeon that saved (the remnants of) the Lost Battalion: and blithely took it to Philadel-

phia and handed it to Mr. Bok. He read it then and there and said he'd take it, and urged me to write more for LHJ [*Ladies' Home Journal*]: I said thank you, no, I wanted to go back to San Francisco: he argued that I could do that and still write for LHJ: I could, he said, commute. I said no, I did not like New York, I thought the Atlantic far inferior to the Pacific. "Think it over; think it over," he said as we parted.

Berta and I discussed it for a couple of weeks, and even dreamed on the bedspring about how much LHJ would pay for that piece: we decided. $50. And privately I thought of $75, but suppressed that thought to prevent being disappointed . . .. The envelope came: with flopping hands, while Berta held her breath, I opened it, check for $750. My God, we were so rich that I didn't write another word all that spring.[65]

One of Berta's new assignments that winter was a children's page for *McCall's*. The first one appeared in February, with a Valentine's Day theme, possibly inspired by the decorated letters Elmer was sending her from France. The page had various sized hearts and included detailed instructions about cutting them out and putting them together to make valentine cards. She used the pen name of Barbara Hale to distinguish these children's pages from her more serious work.

Elmer was mustered out of the army in February 1919, and he and Berta finally had the joyous reunion they'd dreamed of for so long. Quarters for the returning soldier were arranged on the top floor of the Jones Street house, and they began to make plans for their future. Their original plans were to return to San Francisco, but many of their old Telegraph Hill friends were settling in New York.

Elmer knew his back pay for military service wouldn't last long, and if they stayed, Berta could continue her steady work for *McCall's*. He'd received one assignment for an oil portrait, but the war had caused the market for fine art to dry up. Still, there seemed to be more paying art opportunities in New York than in San Francisco, so they decided to stay in the east. He'd had some assignments from *Asia* magazine, illustrating some of Frederick O'Brien's *South Seas Stories*, edited by Rose Wilder Lane. Editors Edith and Gertrude Emerson usually published four or five of his sketches per story, and he received credit on the masthead.[66] Other illustrating jobs came along, and he enjoyed accompanying Berta to zoos and circuses for illustration ideas,[67] but he hoped to find more fulfilling work.[68]

They quickly decided on a wedding date: 14 July. They also needed a place of their own. And, spoiled by life on Telegraph Hill, they insisted on having a view. They began their search in Greenwich Village. It was becoming popular with the "uptown crowd: that group of society who finds pleasure in the 'bohemian' atmosphere created by workers in the arts, which meant the rents began to soar."[69] Berta and Elmer searched the village thoroughly. Nothing they could afford. They decided to start at the southernmost point of Manhattan and work their way north. Fortunately it was a mild spring.

Elmer wrote later about their search for a place to live. ". . . In the aftermath of war, the need for housing became acute . . . .. There were thousands of returning soldiers anxious to marry and establish a home and family. All building materials were short and in great demand. Plumbing and electrical supplies were at all-time highs. High wages made the erection of even a very small home an expensive proposition. Speculation in land became the order of the day and land values forced prices higher and higher."[70] However, he had learned in the army and after the earthquake, not to "wince at disaster." Something would always turn up.

They covered Manhattan by subway and on foot. "The only empty places offered no view; only blank walls or the neighbors' wash greeted the eye."[71] Up by Spuyten Duyvil they found some empty houses needing repair and with neglected gardens. There were views of the Hudson and the distant Palisades. Their hopes rose. It would be perfect.

Hopes fell when they learned the houses were to be torn down for Washington Park.

In spite of the seeming impossibility of finding a place that was just what they wanted, they kept up their search northward along the river and through Westchester County. "We felt sure that somewhere near New York there must be a small house or a barn that could be made into a studio or living quarters. After each day's search we returned to the city and worked on art ideas to sell to magazines. The day for our marriage was rapidly approaching and as of yet we had no place to go."[72]

Someone suggested Sneden's Landing, a tiny village on the west side of the river, so they took the train up to Dobbs Ferry and took a small boat across the river to the western shore. This was the first time they'd ever seen the famous Palisades from river level and the towering cliffs impressed them.[73] They could see the village was too well kept to be affordable but felt the quiet of this village off the beaten path was a bit of heaven. The air was sweet with the warm fragrance of gardens in bloom and filled with the song and twitter of birds. Rounding a sharp turn in the steep road they came to a latticed gate set in a whitewashed stonewall.[74]

This lovely spot was owned by Mary Lawrence Tonetti. She had been a sculptor and protégé of Augustus Saint-Gaudens, and had, like Elmer, studied at the Académie Julian[75] before marrying sculptor Joseph Tonetti. She offered them a log cabin that could be made into a studio, but they didn't want to wait for completion. Mrs. Tonetti suggested they walk through the woods to Piermont, and then follow River Road to Nyack.

It was a pleasant walk, past many substantial Dutch houses built of the region's red sandstone. They went through some shady woods, and then the quiet of the morning was broken suddenly by the sound of many dogs barking. Rounding a corner they found a two-story house, with dogs barking from every window. They stopped to ask a man sitting under a tree if they were on the road to Nyack. The dogs were so deafening he couldn't hear the question, so he said "shut up " in a very quiet tone of voice. The sudden quiet was startling. The dogs in the window openings disappeared from view. He told them the dogs were boarders and many would be taken to pet stores in the city. The idea of giving a dwelling over to dogs in the middle of a housing crisis upset Berta, since so many people, including themselves, needed a home.

They continued down the road, enjoying the trees, flowers, and wide blue skies, and looking for rent or sale signs. The road skirted the foot of a mountain and ran beside a pretty creek. The two became more and more convinced they were not meant to be city dwellers and could easily understand why the region was considered a painters' paradise.

Piermont blended imperceptibly into the adjoining village of Grand View-on-Hudson. We walked past house after house. Some large, some small, all occupied, none for sale, none for rent . . . There was nothing to mar the serenity and beauty of the homes nestling on the hillside. We sat for a moment's rest on a stone wall where we could see the broad sweep of the river . . . the war had put a complete stop to yachting and only now were sails beginning to reappear on the river.

The village . . . reminded us both of Telegraph Hill in San Francisco. At this point the Hudson was almost as wide as San Francisco Bay. The ridge rising from the river, though covered with woods that hid most of the houses, was scarred with quarries like Telegraph Hill. Tarrytown, directly across the river, made a good substitute for the cities across the bay, and the hills of Westchester were not unlike the Berkeley Hills. The scene lacked only Mount Tamalpais and the slow drifting summer fog to complete the resemblance.[76]

They kept walking past charming old houses and a wild piece of acreage thick with blackberries, squirrels, and chattering jays. They finally found food at the old Hotel St. George in the village of South Nyack. The rest and food convinced them both that this charming village on the river had everything they wanted in the way of a home site.

An "affable" agent staffed the only real estate office in town. Berta and Elmer told him they wanted a house either on the river or with a river view, with a modest price or rent. He said he understood but then drove them around to many unsuitable places far from the river. Finally, he confessed he had nothing on his list that matched what they wanted. Berta mentioned seeing a man fixing the roof of an old house in Grand View. Maybe he'd know if it was for sale or rent.

The agent thought he knew the place. "You mean the old Lyall Hotel? There's no heat in the place. Must have been the owner you saw working."[77] He took them there, saying that before the war it had been a summer hotel known for its wonderful meals.

The owner silently appraised the eager young couple. Apparently satisfied, he agreed to rent the place for $25 a month after the roof was fixed. He was not interested in a long-term lease and trusted Elmer for the rent, saying he believed a man was as good as his word.

Success! They'd found their place on the Hudson River. Now they could get married.

CHAPTER THREE

TWO PATHS THE SAME

One love, one aim/two paths the same.
Hold fast . . . and love will last.

– Anonymous

Berta and Elmer could hardly believe their luck. Now they had a place in the country with plenty of room for all their friends to visit. Gleefully, they announced to all their friends that they had rented a large old hotel with plenty of room for anyone who cared to visit them once they married.[78] They'd leave Jones Street as soon as the marriage took place. Rose decided to leave Jones Street as well, and rent a small room in Croton-on-Hudson where she planned to concentrate on finishing her work on O'Brien's *White Shadows in the South Seas*.[79] She would get a fee of $500 on publication and a third of any royalties it earned. Then she'd begin her planned biography of Herbert Hoover.

The next item on the Haders' agenda was getting the marriage license. They had to go to City Hall to obtain one. Later *Asia* editor Gertrude Emerson wrote, "Berta, as you know, had a sweet shyness. They didn't know exactly where to go and stopped to ask a policeman near the spot. Berta said innocently, 'we want to get a car license . . .. Can you tell us where to go?' The policeman, recognizing them for what they were and not blinking an eyelash, told them to go into the building, to such and such a floor, to room number such and such."[80] They followed his directions and were quite surprised to find his directions led to the marriage license bureau. They filled out the application carefully. Elmer used their new home in Nyack as his legal address.

Both wanted the simplest wedding possible. Another old friend, Eve Chappel, wrote that Berta couldn't bear the thought of a regular church ritualistic thing, either in church or at home, and she was just as averse to a Justice of the Peace ordeal, and yet she wanted something by way of a ceremony. She was unable to see why she couldn't just sign something and have it over.[81]

As usual, Bessie Beatty took charge. The wedding would be on Monday, 14 July, at a tea in her apartment, and the only guests would be old California friends plus one or two others, including a Kenneth Durant who had just bought a nice tea tray in Chinatown.[82] She arranged for the "signing" to be conducted by Tyler Dennett, a journalist and former minister she had met through John Rockefeller's Interchurch World Movement. Rose and Bessie would serve as witnesses. [83]

Berta planned to wear her suit. Saturday night before the wedding, she decided she'd better wash her white blouse before the big occasion. Bessie decided Berta should have a wedding dress, and found some white silk shantung in one of her trunks.

Rose, who'd learned her needle working skills from her grand-mother and blind Aunt Mary,[84] offered to embroider a colorful trim on both the smock and skirt so it would look gay instead of bridal. They found a store still open where they purchased thread and embroidery floss, and the three spent all the next day making the dress and embroidering wide bands of color around the hem of the smock and sleeves.[85] They were still embroidering it the day of the wedding. By five o'clock the dress was almost finished and Eve hurriedly basted in the sleeves. They gathered at Bessie's for the official ceremony. Stella Karn, a San Francisco friend who did pub-licity for the Interchurch organization, had arrived early to help with the cakes and tiny sandwiches. When she realized Berta was wearing a dress, not a suit, Stella decided to do the same. In her usual impulsive fashion she ran outside, climbed into a taxi before the man who had ordered it could do so, and tore home to change into a lavender organdy dress.[86]

Berta got her wish for an almost minimal ceremony. Eve de-scribed it this way:

> We got the sleeves in. And the guests came. And the clergyman. Then he and Elmer and Berta sat down to a little mahogany desk, and he asked them whether they would love and cherish each other, and I had to dash out to get a pin because one of Berta's sleeves was coming out. It was one wedding at which no tears were shed. And, comicly [sic] as it sounds, it was really beautiful. They are an adorable pair.[87]

When Berta began objecting to anything in the ceremony be-sides the "I dos", Elmer finally told Bessie to "Make Berta behave!" Berta, wanting to get it over with, then agreed to everything that the minister said. It was so minimal that an army friend of Elmer's who had dropped in kept conversing in another corner, never noticing what was going on.[88] One guest was unsure if they really were married!

Their honeymoon would be at the Lyall Hotel, and their honeymoon trip would be traveling the 25 miles to Nyack. They took a train from Grand Central Station up to Tarrytown with most of their belongings and the two Jones Street cats yowling in a basket. They crossed to Nyack on the red-painted ferryboat, along with a band of gypsies. Colorfully dressed women and men with many wild-looking children filled a collection of jalopies. Others walked around the boat, looking for fortune-telling customers. One exotic looking young gypsy matron picked Elmer as a likely prospect.

> Failing in her attempt to persuade me to put my wallet in her hands for a blessing, she seized my hand and quickly placed it against warm bare skin on a bare midriff just above her skirt line. Then she belched and informed me she had swallowed all my bad luck. Nothing but happiness lay before me. I hastily crossed her extended palm with a fifty-cent piece and in some embarrassment broke away from the diviner of the future and joined my bride who had been a rather interested spectator of the proceedings.[89]

The gypsy blessing, dismissed at the time, must have had more power than they thought. The Lyall Hotel in Grand View-on-Hudson provided a happy start to married life and continuing contact with old friends. Berta and Elmer had told everyone that "The hospitality of the old Lyall Hotel was about to be rekindled. Not as a business but as a retreat for our friends . . . Jolly weekends . . . after a necessary amount of art work had been done to bring in the rent money and pay for the groceries."

A few joined them on their first honeymoon weekend. As El-mer said later when writing about these years, "they were all art-ists and writers who wouldn't mind the lack of furnishings: each would decorate in his own mind just how the place would look when we got around to fixing it up." Their funds would stretch to one good fifty-dollar mattress, or five "not so good" ten-dollar ones.[90] They bought the cheap ones, so they could have visitors right away. A painter guest who tagged along with other friends "spent his first few hours helping his host make a bed of 2x3 pine studs so that he would have a place to sleep."[91]

The long days of summer on the Tappan Zee[92] were perfect for honeymooners. Elmer describes listening to the soft lap of the water on the sandy shore, and feeling the east wind whipping the surface into a patchwork of white caps. After busy days and weeks they found time to sit on the dock and watch the sunsets, appreci-ate restful twilight, and enjoy the music that wafted in from Satur-day night dances at the Yacht Club next door. Even the inevitable mosquitoes seemed tolerable.

Their friends liked getting away from the bustle to spend weekends at what was soon dubbed "Lyall Cottage." Those who had been overseas during the stressful days of the war—Bessie Beatty, Guy Moyston, Will Irwin, Rose Wilder Lane—must have en-joyed the peaceful setting in Grand View-on-Hudson. Old friends brought new friends to share the weekends. Columnist Floyd Dell said that "nearly everyone you meet says 'I'm going out to Elmer's and Berta's this weekend. Want to come along? They'd love to have you.'[93]" When Dell finally visited he sat enchanted, listening as another visitor told stories about the fabulous Moorish life on the Island of Majorca, just off Spain. Part of the fun was never knowing for sure who would be around and getting to know former strangers. Hamilton Williamson was a friend of Frank Buck, a noted animal collector who specialized in bringing wild animals from exotic places to America, and she had many stories to tell. She came often with her son, Toby Carroll.

Though the former hotel was old, they were young and adaptable. Originally they slept on pallets on the floor[94] but later a large third-floor room with gorgeous views of the Hudson was turned into a women's dorm. Elmer built box-like supports for the bedding around the sides. One woman fell into the cellar after stepping on a loose floorboard, but since she wasn't hurt, it became just another story to tell.

There was only one bathroom, so both men and women lined up outside in the morning, towels over their arms and toothbrushes in hands.[95] They paddled up and down the river in the newly acquired second-hand canoe, swam in the Hudson at high tide, or hiked up the South Mountain ridge.

Mary Margaret McBride, a newspaper woman whom Rockefeller hired to do public relations for the Interchurch World Movement, met the Haders through Stella Karn. McBride wrote later that, "It is sad to be without kinfolk or a special place that seems like home in a big lonely city at times like Christmas or Thanksgiving—holidays that need a special sort of celebration. That sort of desolation can never come to the Haders' friends, for ever since their marriage they have been family to a group of some forty intimates without close ties in this part of the world. These lucky men and women have standing engagements each year."[96]

They also had to cope with the vagaries of hosts who cherished all living beings, even spiders. Lyall Cottage had big windows looking out on the river, and "Elwell the spider" built a web inside one. The Haders fed him flies, thought the web a work of art and said spiders bring good fortune and Elwell brought them luck. The weekenders were always willing to help with chores, and one day Hamilton Williamson decided to dust the house while the Haders were out in their canoe. Berta looked up to see Hamilton's dust cloth coming closer and closer to Elwell's web. She frantically waved her hands and yelled to "Spare Elwell," but her words couldn't penetrate the window. Elwell and the web of art disappeared forever into the dust cloth.

When Katherine Anne Porter and some of the others realized Berta was washing all the sheets by hand, they organized a secret Christmas gift. Somehow, they smuggled in a large washing machine without Berta's knowledge. She was totally surprised and promptly named it "Abraham Lincoln" because it freed the slaves!

Saturday night suppers were basic and simple, usually polenta along with a big green salad. Berta had learned to make good soup and inexpensive filling meals from her Telegraph Hill neighbors. There might be cauldrons of fish and meat stews made from cheap cuts of meat, gnocchi, baked beans, and spaghetti.[97] She undoubtedly used some of Elmer's mother's recipes: Lena Hader had traded recipes with other immigrants as she traveled across the country,[98] as well as using recipes from her native Sweden. One of Elmer's favorites was a spicy Swedish prune soup, served to the King of Sweden when he visited the United States. When Willy Pogany brought his sister Paula to visit, Berta learned how to cook Hungarian stuffed cabbage. Paula also provided other tasty and inexpensive recipes to add to the weekend fare. (Later Paula published her own Hungarian cookbook.[99])

Other dishes depended on what the guests brought. Butter was expensive, but margarine, colored with the contents of a yellow dye capsule enclosed in every package, was a fair substitute. Stella Karn loved exploring different areas of the city and often brought exotic treats from foreign markets, to go with her more practical offerings of a ham or leg of lamb.[100]

Elmer had always been an early riser, full of plans for the coming day. He liked to plan his weeks as well. Daily life in Grand View soon fell into a predictable pattern. Monday was "get acquainted day" to learn about their new hometown and township. They walked the two miles into Nyack's shopping center and back, checking every house along the route to see if one might be available permanently. Tuesday and Wednesday they worked at their desks and drawing boards. Berta continued her regular work for *McCall's*, including the children's pages. Besides the special holiday projects, she added paper dolls, which were very well received. Her fashion eye probably influenced some of the clothing.

The *McCall's* children's pages led to many others in the popular magazines. Busy parents appreciated having a project to keep the children occupied, while they themselves read the stories and articles in peace. Berta and Elmer had each grown up creating their own toys out of any available items, and it was easy to share these ideas.

Berta once said that when they were working in their separate art fields, miniature and impressionist paintings, neither would have dreamed of touching each other's work.[101] Now they joined their childhood memories and artistic talents into designing easily crafted paper toys, showcasing silly clowns, fairy tale characters, and children from other lands. These fun projects were now attributed jointly to Berta and Elmer Hader.[102]

Paper dolls were a perennial favorite of the time. Readers loved the Haders' "Toddling Tootsies," plump, rosy-faced children with colorful clothes. Besides the static paper figure, though, the Haders' paper figures were also educational. One series showed children from around the world, each boy and girl depicted in native costume. Small tabs enabled children to fasten the dolls into the landscape of the foreign country.

They also designed figures that could be cut out and fastened together with simple brads, enabling them to be moved around to become more of an active toy. *Sunshine House, The Children's Happy House* ran as a serial project in 1924 issues of *McCall's*: each month a different room in the house was a background for the paper dolls. When put together the little paper figures could be placed in different rooms.

Their shoebox "peep shows," based on common folk tales, had detailed instructions for assembling, lighting, and performing. It took time and skill to cut out the many small figures carefully and paste them into the proper places. However, once finished, the child could peek through a hole in one end of the shoebox and see a complete three-dimensional fairy tale scene. This was also something that could be shown off to visiting relatives or neighbors.

Then Berta and Elmer created a "finger doll" that could dance around using the child's fingers as the doll's legs. There were little shoes for the fingers along with the clothing and the directions were shown in the heading at the top of the page. Elmer later wrote the directions out for printer Charles Stringer, who was thinking about putting the dolls on the back of cereal boxes.

Thursdays they took the train into the city, delivered their finished work, and then made the rounds of magazine editors in search of more work to do. On Fridays they cleaned house and prepared for guests.[103]

Autumn came suddenly. The hills turned color overnight, unlike the West's gradual and subdued changes. They were stunned by their surroundings. "The towering weeping willows and here and there a group of sassafras trees still retaining their green leaves served as accents for the brilliant yellows, scarlets and many tones of red and brown that spread north, south and westward over the hill."[104]

The glorious fall inspired them to take a longer walk one day, up on the ridge and westward toward the farmlands. They admired the glossy red and green leaf clusters of the poison ivy and the brilliance of the scarlet sumac. A woman leading a red and white cow into a barn invited them to sit on her porch and have a refreshing drink of well water. She told the Haders about how, as a widow woman, she made a living on these two acres. She kept up her home, grew and canned her own fruits and vegetables, turned her cow's milk into butter and cheese and sold the surplus to the summer visitors. She had Rhode Island Red chickens providing eggs, a pig in the sty and needed to purchase only a few staples from the store. It sounded idyllic.

Berta and Elmer went back to Lyall Cottage, more determined than ever to find such a home of their own. As they lived and worked in the cottage, they made needed improvements, such as painting the floors, fixing the plumbing, and spading the lawn into a vegetable garden. They invited all their friends for Thanksgiving dinner and were delighted to see representatives of California, Texas, the Deep South, the Midwest, and New England all sitting around the circular dining room table. It was a bit crowded but no one minded. Everyone brought part of the feast and had such fun it became an annual tradition. They missed their many friends who were too far away to join them, and combined talents to send a wonderful and personal Christmas card, which became another annual Hader custom.

The fall had been warm and colorful. The clear winter days had a very different beauty, and inspired Elmer to take out his brushes once again. He painted several winter scenes of River Road before retreating from the shocking cold.

"When a cold Nor'easter blew across the river and began to whistle through the cracks and crevices of the house,"[105] they realized they were living in a summer hotel, not a year round one. The only heat came from the coal-burning kitchen stove, but since all the plumbing ran through that room, they were spared frozen pipes. They used their gas-burning heater until they got the first bill from the gas company and realized it was too costly for daily use. It would have to be saved for emergencies. They finally found a wood-burning Franklin stove in an antique store—they were familiar with these from Telegraph Hill—and set it up in their living room. It heated the large room adequately as long as they kept the sunroom door closed.

"Most of that winter, we sat on chairs by the kitchen coal stove. By placing our feet, encased in felt boots from Sears Roebuck, in the oven of the stove, our raised knees formed an incline upon which to rest our drawing boards."[106] Besides the small items—bookplates, headers for book chapters, book jackets, sketches—Elmer also created some full-color magazine covers, including several for *Metropolitan Magazine.* This was a magazine which published theater reviews, political pieces by well-known personages like Theodore Roosevelt, and stories by Jack London.

Other opportunities came by unexpected routes. George Leonard Sill, editor of *The Christian Science Monitor*, later became a great friend. He liked to tease Elmer and said he was the person who launched Elmer into children's illustrations. Apparently Elmer had added an illustration of an empty squirrel cage to a letter Rose Wilder Lane was sending about the status of her story, and he liked the drawing enough to ask Elmer to illustrate for *The Monitor*. It also led to new additions to the Hader weekend clan: both editor George Sill and his assistant Edythe Kirk (Buckie) Buckminster often visited Grand View in the following years.

The next summer, when the army closed nearby Camp Morris, Berta and Elmer bought a used hot air furnace, came back with a receipted bill and got permission of the owner to install it. Once they finished the work, the owner decided the property was now more desirable. He promptly raised their rent.

When the Hudson froze solidly across to the Westchester shore, Berta and Elmer were thrilled to watch "dozens of skaters, youngsters and oldsters, dotting the ice. Further out were triangular sails, carrying skillful skaters up and down the river with the force of the wind. All artwork ceased for the time being. We took time out to buy skates, and learned to stand upright." Friends from the city came out to enjoy themselves while the ice was in good condition.[107] The winter snows were mostly gone by the middle of March, and Berta, who shared her mother Adelaide's passion for flowers, planted zinnias, nasturtiums, marigolds, bachelor buttons, and petunias to provide a riot of lovely color down to the river. A neighbor gave them a Golden Glow perennial to enliven the front yard.

In 1920 some friends, who'd purchased a 30-acre farm about twelve miles away, brought the Haders over for a visit. Berta and Elmer enjoyed watching them build their house, using the worm-eaten dead chestnut trees as good building material. They were also using red sandstone, or brownstone, to build the house walls—a stone peculiar to the region, fairly easy to work, and long lasting. Many of the early Dutch settler's homes were made of this material. Other city friends were remodeling or building places along the nearby South Mountain Road, but the Haders stubbornly dreamed of a home on a river. They were never satisfied with second best.

Their magazine work began to pick up. The circle of friends grew larger, and a weekend seldom passed without Lyall Cottage being filled. The Partons, Lem, Mary, and daughter Margaret, were now on the East coast, and frequently joined the group on the weekends.

Although the Interchurch World Movement had disbanded, there were hopes that the new League of Nations would bring about world peace. The Bolsheviks had gained power in Russia, and inspired a fear of communism in the United States: 6,000 people were arrested on New Year's Day in 1920. Most were quickly released. However, when two robbers killed a paymaster and absconded with the payroll in Braintree, Massachusetts, the police arrested two young Italian anarchists, Nicola Sacco and Bartolomeo Vanzetti, who spoke very little English. Many felt the men were arrested because of the prejudice against Italians and the current fear of immigrants. Their arrest and conviction caused worldwide protests, including writer Katherine Anne Porter, who often visited Grand View. She, along with poet Edna St. Vincent Millay, had spent hours demonstrating and writing letters in Sacco and Vanzetti's defense. These women were usually arrested by a very polite group of policemen known as the "pink glove squad."[108] Despite all the protests, Sacco and Vanzetti were executed.

Discussions continued to be active. The weekenders were often passionate believers in one side or another, but they held no bitterness toward one another. Women's suffrage was still a hot topic, even though women now had the vote. Most of the group had been and were still suffragettes. Some, like Ernestine Evans, had also been arrested. Those protests and arrests must have sparked major conversation around the Hader table. Most thought that once women had the vote, graft in politics would end. Berta and Elmer consistently opposed violence, were loving, pacific, gentle and tolerant.[109] Berta was gaining a reputation as someone who kept things calm, and one who kept all confidences safe. There was often good news to talk about too. Everyone was thrilled when Freddy O'Brien's book, *White Shadows in the South Seas*, became a best seller, and much credit was given to Rose for her expert editing.

The Haders spent their spare time in the evenings drawing different plans for their dream house. All plans called for a large studio-living room with tall windows on the north and a good sized fireplace. They had the plans for a dwelling, but still no lot on which to build.

When friends suggested the old Revolutionary Spy House across the river might be available, they went to take a look. It was another Old Dutch house, this time with grey stone walls. They liked the house and considered its proportions perfect, so they measured the length and height of the building and the walls. They even sketched floor plans and window placements and noted the framework of hand-hewed chestnut.

The owner didn't think the house was worth much, but it stood in the middle of 50 acres valued at one thousand dollars an acre. That was way too expensive, and when they went back to the owner, hoping he would let them at least salvage the framework, the owner said he had decided to remodel the house using the Haders' own plans as they had described them. It was no longer for sale.

In spite of these disappointments, life in the old hotel went along smoothly. Berta accepted a design position with the Ukrainian Needleworkers Guild, organized to help immigrant women make money with their sewing skills. They needed the extra money, though it meant commuting back and forth to the city. Working hard during the week and entertaining city friends on weekends left them little time to take part in village life but the neighbors didn't expect it; they considered anybody who would rent such a rundown building to be a bit crazy.

They were delighted when they discovered a new arrival to the household was expected in the spring. They had always wanted to have a family. They decided the glass-enclosed sunroom would make a more pleasant place to welcome the baby than a hospital room, and Berta preferred to deliver at home. Her doctor agreed. The young expectant parents scrubbed all the woodwork and the floor and sterilized everything they could think of. They found and engaged a nurse to take care of mother and child the first week after the eagerly awaited birth. They were ready for the next step in their lives: parenthood.

Shortly before her due date, her doctor told her that although he had to be away when the baby was due, they shouldn't worry—he had arranged for a substitute doctor to take over. So on 8 March 1921, there was "a day of rejoicing in the house on the river. The baby boy was warmly welcomed as the first baby in our widening circle of friends."[110]

Unfortunately, Berta became deathly ill after the baby's arrival. Elmer always blamed it on the errors of the substitute doctor, but it meant they could never have another child. Theirs would be a one child family. Fortunately, little Hamilton Hader, named after friend and author Hamilton Williamson, was a healthy child.

The nurse stayed on for six more weeks to help Berta recover her strength, but even when the nurse left, Berta was still quite frail. Artist Ernest Haskell and wife Emma, old San Francisco friends, suggested the new little family leave their usual hustle and bustle, rent out Lyall Cottage, and spend the summer recuperating at the Haskell's home in West Point, Maine.[111]

It was just what they needed. In the peace and quiet of the Maine coast, Berta recovered her strength and became able to care for their strapping son. The picturesque coast inspired Elmer, and he found time to pick up his oils. He created enough "West Point, Maine" paintings for an exhibit the following summer.

They returned to Lyall Cottage, ready to start back to work and enthusiastic about the future. Hammie developed into a happy baby with a disposition that endeared him to all his parents' friends. Now they had another good reason to find a permanent residence.

A large manor house on a plateau across the road from the yacht club had a good view of the river. The owner wasn't interested in selling the property. However, she thought her sister, who owned the one untamed piece of property in the village, might be. It was on a steep hill considered so unbuildable that no one had ever offered to buy it. The northern part of the lot ran back to the high wall of an old brownstone quarry, while the southern half was marshy and full of springs. It was covered thickly with weeds, myrtle, sumac, brambles, elderberry bushes, and "criss-crossed blackberries."

Berta and Elmer had noticed the property from the first day, enjoying its variety of bird life. They felt confident that somewhere on that piece of wild hillside they could find space for a house. After all, they had seen houses in San Francisco hung on hillsides just as steep. They talked to the sister.

After seeing their enthusiasm and hearing their plans, she was willing to sell to them. They had just signed a contract for a new children's feature page so felt they could afford to buy one-half of the property. They chose the southern part that had a spring feeding a small meandering stream which disappeared under the road and reemerged as a brook tumbling down to the Hudson. The owner quoted a reasonable price and offered to draw up all the necessary papers herself since she was a law school graduate. No agent would be involved.

They didn't have enough money in the bank to buy all the property, even though their prospects were good. But the seller was eager to help this young couple obtain their dream. She asked Elmer to paint her portrait as a partial payment. Their passion for the property persuaded Bessie Beatty to buy the property, and they would repay the loan to her. They finally had their dream place with a view of the river.

When their landlord heard about the purchase, he remarked, "Hader is a fool. Nobody can build on that land. It would take a million dollars to get it in shape for a lawn and a garden."[112] Berta and Elmer paid no heed. They had no intention of putting in a fine lawn and formal garden. They liked the overgrown lot just the way it was.

✦ CHAPTER FOUR ✦

WILLOW HILL

Now all they had to do was clear the lot, select a spot for the house, and then build it. Elmer firmly believed that anyone could build a home. "Rodents do it. So do birds. And squirrels." So could they.

Elmer had done well in shop classes in school, and had remodeled his parents' attic into a studio. His friends appreciated his ability to build things over the years. Berta, convinced Elmer was able to do anything, was determined they could tame the jungle. They had little money but plenty of friends who were equally enthusiastic about a new and improved weekend destination. Writer and businesswoman Hamilton Williamson cautioned them first to have enough money in their budget and then allow for a third more than they thought. That advice was so discouraging they didn't make a budget. They figured they'd build as they could afford it.

When the spring of 1922 finally arrived, they bought a sickle, hatchet, axe, and honing stone and began slowly cutting a path through the tangles of blackberry, elderberry, and sumac. The sumac was so rampant Elmer found it hard to believe the neighboring landscaper when he said sumac was prized in England and found only in the finest gardens. It was hard to destroy.

The weekend friends would arrive on the "jerky little Erie train almost every Saturday afternoon after work was ended (we had a six-day week of course), get out at the small station of Grand View, and walk down the rocky hill."[113] After donning overalls, they set out to attack the overgrowth and haul stones into piles for later use. "More accustomed to pencil, paint brushes, or the typewriter than pick and shovel, all quickly developed blisters on hands and lame backs."[114] Ernestine Evans, Elsie Weil, and Gertrude Emerson, *Asia Magazine* journalists, were intrepid travelers and keen observers of how people lived and worked in unusual places. Later on they would found the extant Society of Women Geographers, but now they were getting real world experience in building a house by hand. Berta sometimes came down from the house with Hammie to help, but the baby and the artwork took most of her time.

Mary Margaret McBride said her only contribution was to sit on a boulder, watch them all work, and hand out fudge for quick energy. But most of the group enjoyed the physical effort as a change from sitting in a chair. Lem and Mary Parton, Katherine Anne Porter, and Toby Carroll all had the time, energy, and boundless enthusiasm to come out every weekend and help get rid of the brush. The only casualty among all these amateur brush pullers was a cut finger on little Margaret Parton, Lem and Mary's daughter, who wouldn't listen to Berta's advice on how to use a sickle.

There was way too much brush to figure out where the house could sit. The sloping land had many small hills and valleys, and willows were everywhere. The weekenders started calling the lot "Willow Hill." Assorted boulders and stone slabs from the quarry were scattered about. These were gathered in piles for eventual use as building material. The land was also marshy. When, in late summer, they finally slashed a path up the hill, they discovered an old springhouse. Apparently the spring had once furnished water to several nearby houses before the city water system was established.[115] Water still rushed out of an iron pipe, creating a small stream that wound its way down to the base of the property.

Above the springhouse was a 30-foot "cup-shaped hollow." When they burned off the sumac and cleared the space, they found a large pile of variously sized stones. The space looked fairly flat and suitable for building, and the lay of the land solved many excavating problems: Elmer decided he could take advantage of the dips in the land and build trenches between them for the foundation. The site was relatively private and had a great view of the Hudson.

The next step was getting the building materials. The war had depleted supplies, so they were often found in out of the way places. And, once found, how could they be delivered? The Haders usually walked to town and back. The Piermont to Nyack bus was undependable. Baldy, the postman, provided most delivery service, using a mail cart looking like a "derby box on wheels" [116] pulled by faithful horse Nellie.

A neighbor offered to sell them his 1914 "Apperson Jackrabbit" touring car.[117]

They purchased it for $75, with arrangements to leave it in the owner's garage for the winter—that would give them plenty of time to build their own garage before the spring. Wanting to keep the river views unspoiled, they chose a garage site 150 feet from the main road, never thinking about shoveling snow or coping with the effect of frost or spring thaws. They planned an inexpensive garage, built of wood siding and covered with stucco, and sent for the booklets on materials supplied by large lumber companies. Elmer pored over the tools illustrated in the mail order catalogs.

By watching stonemasons at work on nearby buildings, they learned how to mix cement and lay a foundation with the sandstone. As they were ready to build the walls, it seemed a shame to waste the site's view on just a garage—why not build it so it could also be used as a studio? Elmer immediately changed the plans, beginning his famous tradition of constantly improvising his home. He changed "the flat roof to a high-peaked gable, put a tall studio window in the north wall, and a fireplace in the center of the south one."[118] They covered the wooden sidewalls with heavy tarpaper. So far, so good.

There was abundant quarry stone to use for the fireplace. Professional masons were expensive, so they hired John and Rocco, two Italians who could lay a good stonewall, even though unable to read an architect's plan. Communicating with them was difficult, but they taught Elmer how to make a mortar box and mix quantities of mortar and how to use tools such as stone hammers, plumbs, and levels. While the workmen stopped work at the end of an eight-hour day, the Haders carried on until dark, in spite of stone bruises and blisters. The last task of the day was to raise the scaffolding around the growing chimney so all would be in readiness when the masons showed up for work the following day.[119]

The Italians insisted the flue should get smaller as it grew taller. Sometime earlier, when the Haders looked at fireplaces, they had met an old Swede known as the "fireplace doctor." He made a living by keeping architect designed fireplaces from smoking. Maybe, they thought, the workmen were "chimney doctors" who knew what they were doing.

As soon as the chimney was finished, the Haders inscribed the date in the cement and then eagerly went down to light their first fire. As Elmer noted, "The flames shot up the open throat. We smiled our relief and the two Italians looked at us with wide smiles that said plainly, 'we knew it would work.' Before our smiles were dry on our faces, smoke began to come out of the fireplace opening, first in wisps and then in quantities."[120]

The Italians peered up into the throat and shook their heads. They walked outside, looked at the high chimney, and shook their heads. The Haders were sure it was the too small chimney flue that caused "the obnoxious smoking," but decided not to worry about it until after the garage became a studio cottage. It wouldn't be needed till then, and the steep roof had to be shingled before winter.

A salesman in a local hardware store knew how to lay asphalt shingles and volunteered to help on the weekend. The work went quickly. When they reached the chimney and needed copper flashing, they "ad libbed" with strips of tin cut from empty cans. By quitting time on Sunday, the roof was almost finished.

Then it was time to stucco the walls, and the Italians said they would help with the first scratch coat. The Haders remembered the cheerful effect of the colored stucco houses in San Francisco and decided to use pink stucco on the garage. This was uncommon in New York. So they wrote to a cement company to find out how and what, went into the city for materials, and hired an experienced mason for the finish coat. Since no one had ever used the coloring powder, Berta and Elmer followed instructions and mixed it themselves. Once on the wall, it looked liver-colored. They hastily reduced the amount of color. When the cement dried, the walls were a lighter pink than they had wanted, but they decided to keep them that way.

They hired a local electrician to install a few outlets, and he showed them how to "install outlet boxes, cut armored cable, splice wires, and run cable through the studding. This money was well-spent, too."[121] Their landlord volunteered to help install the stock windows and doors—a simple operation except the two windows were a half-inch different and the landlord sawed the half-inch off the smaller one. Elmer rebuilt the windows and painted the trim and doors a light green. The finished building looked very attractive among the bright fall foliage. A garage-less neighbor offered them $10 a month to rent the space, and they settled down to garnering assignments and creating magazine pages during the winter, well-pleased with the summer's achievements.

When spring banished the last vestiges of snow from the hillside, they decided to make use of the Jackrabbit. A garage man had installed a large battery in the car, and a neighbor offered to drive it from the storage barn to the Haders' new garage. Unfortunately, the previous owner had not drained the radiator, and the engine was a solid block of ice after the cold winter. The battery almost tore the engine apart when it turned the motor over.[122]

Once the Jackrabbit was fixed and sitting in their dirt driveway, the Haders set about learning how to drive. As usual, they studied a book on the workings of the gas engine. Each learned to start the car, back it up, and stop the engine. After a little practice, they got their drivers' licenses from the county clerk and drove around the country looking for such things as supplies for sale and old buildings being taken down—good sources for almost free lumber and hardware.

During the winter, they'd begun to plan the house they hoped to build in spring. They wanted a large living room with many windows, a large fireplace, and a small kitchen requiring an "economy of effort." The upstairs would have two bedrooms and bath under a high gable with peaked unbroken rooflines.

The "weekenders" had continued to come through the winter months. Little Hammie was the only child in the whole bunch and a pet for all. He learned the names of every visitor, while Berta and Elmer did their best to keep him from being spoiled. He learned early not to be possessive about the gifts he received but always to acknowledge the giver.

Like most new mothers, Berta followed the current medical advice about frequent checkups for babies. Every time they went in to New York for their work, she took Hammie in to the doctor. He was a very healthy baby.

Besides admiring the baby, the friends also made suggestions for the house. One suggested a flatter roof would give them larger bedrooms but they preferred the picturesque to the practical. They decided on a house 26' wide and 36' long, with the gable end parallel with the north-south River Road below. Elmer found a book by architect Ernest Flagg with many new and interesting ideas on small houses.[123] A method of wall building seemed feasible, as did Flagg's recommendation of omitting cellars as useless damp spaces. They built a small model to scale from an empty fruit crate and used illustration board for the roof. As they worked with the model, they expanded it to include wings on each side of the building. The north wing would contain a studio, with a very high window to capture the north light.

Between preparing new magazine pages, taking care of little Hammie, and the usual household chores, the Haders' winter went by quickly.

By April 1923, the days were lengthening enough that work on the house could begin in earnest. Elmer began rising at 5 a.m. to work on the lot until an 8 a.m. breakfast and then get back to his illustrating work. Birds sang along while he built a 3-foot long trench, 2-foot wide, in his first three hour shift, using the dirt to fill in hollow spots outside the wall line, and adding the rocks from the trench to the pile of building stone. Since there were as many rocks in the ground as above it, he knew they'd have plenty of stone for building. He also realized the 30-foot building they'd planned would require excavating into the slope.

Toby Carroll came out most weekends for the exercise. He helped cut down bramble and sumac around the planned foundation. Although spring rains made work slow with the heavy earth sticking to the shovel, there were clear mornings as well. Then Berta would put the baby in the pushcart and come over to the lot to inspect the completed work. When the 8:11 commuter train whistle blew, Elmer quit work and the small family enjoyed a peaceful and quiet walk back to Lyall Cottage.

Elmer worked daily on his three-hour morning shift, either cutting trenches or sifting the removed dirt through screening to save the small stones for future drainage. He found more slabs of good building stone in the ground and added them to the building pile. However, one large rock ledge could not be removed without blasting. Elmer was afraid blasting might "pinch" or stop the spring from flowing, so he decided to use the ledge as part of the foundation.

By May the briars all rejuvenated themselves, and he stabbed a finger on a blackberry thorn. It caused a painful infection. The doctor who lanced it told him to stay away from clearing brush. He went back to his desk and finished some overdue magazine pages. The following Wednesday he took them into the city. On the way he stopped by the apartment of Gertrude Emerson and Elsie Weil, gave them some fresh violets, and checked on a roof platform they'd asked him to build. When asked about Hammie, Elmer reported he had a slight touch of fever.[124]

On his return home, he was stunned to find two doctors consulting over Hammie. The touch of fever had become extremely serious. It turned out to be spinal meningitis. There was no cure. He was rushed to a New York City hospital, but nothing could be done. Their lively and beloved little son—the only child they would ever be able to have—was gone in only four days. Gertrude reported the violets Elmer had brought were still fresh when they received the news of his death—it seemed impossible Hammie had left them that quickly.

Berta and Elmer were devastated. How could they go on living and working for a house that Hammie would not share? They couldn't even concentrate on the illustration work that paid the bills.

Berta's mother, Adelaide, wrote to her, reminding her of the loss of her father when she was only five.

> You have a deep and abiding something that
> has always been your strength. I remember

when your father passed away and we went back into the empty rooms, it was lonely and desolate. Little as you were, I spoke to you of it and you said 'I am not lonely. God came and took my papa and some day he will come for us and that is all there is.' So, for you perhaps the great spirit of life shadows you and gives you the courage and the faith that we must all have to go on."[125]

It had been an astute comment for a five-year-old to make, and obviously her mother had found it so comforting she'd treasured the words forever. Now she hoped to pass the comfort to her daughter.

Friends, who also had loved Hammie, also rallied around offering needed sympathy and support. Bessie Beatty, as usual, came up with a practical solution and arranged for another peaceful sojourn in Maine. She realized they needed to recover by themselves, without the constant pressure of weekend hosting and house building. They worked through their sadness together in the island peace, and the fresh Atlantic air helped soothe their troubled minds. They returned in the fall with enough energy to plant a vegetable garden, and found working in the soil curative and quieting. Their weekend friends, who'd shared their grief, were delighted to welcome them back to Grand View.

Life would never be the same. They knew it, and their friends knew it. But Berta and Elmer had grown up in times when losses were common. Her mother, Adelaide Hoerner, had survived losing her husband at a young age. Elmer and his family had lost everything they owned in the San Francisco earthquake. But life had gone on. So though they mourned privately, they determined to continue together on their planned life paths.

They were even able to continue the tradition of the big Thanksgiving dinners in Lyall Cottage. Getting back to their usual patterns with old friends who cared was very healing. Life might never be the same for Berta and Elmer, but they were moving on, keeping their sorrow to themselves.

GREETINGS
BERTA + ELMER
· HADER ·

CHAPTER FIVE

AD LIBBING THE LITTLE STONE HOUSE

*Y*ears later, when the Haders were being interviewed by Mary Margaret McBride, Mary Margaret accused them of "ad libbing" their house. Elmer protested: he'd drawn up house plans ahead of time. Berta pointed out those plans were for a house built in a meadow and so didn't work on their steep lot. The entire house was improvised as they dealt with the unexpected. "Ad libbing" was the order of the day.[126]

By the following April (1924), Elmer went back to digging trenches, hoping to get them finished before the summer heat and humidity. They'd paid off their mortgage before Bessie Beatty left for a magazine assignment in England and now owned the lot free and clear. The scale model of their packing crate plan fit their chosen site well.

Berta was noted as a lover of all living things. Friend Elsie Weil called her "Tree Woman." Berta couldn't stand to see a tree cut down, and there were big ones growing on the spot selected for the house. She was upset that a black ash had to be removed from the site of the kitchen door, but they saved the largest pignut tree in the neighborhood by offsetting the studio. A towering elm determined the location of the northeast corner of the house. In hindsight, Berta admitted her insistence on saving trees was a big mistake—most eventually died anyway, and many of their rooms wound up smaller than originally planned.

Just above their chosen site was the brow of the hill, where they could put a small tool shed to protect their newly acquired tools and keep the cement dry. The local lumber company delivered their orders for two by fours, siding, and tar paper and stacked them neatly under a chestnut tree near the road. All of these had to be carried up to where the tool shed would be. Elmer didn't find it too much of a load on the first few trips, but later wrote, "Each trip took longer, rests became more frequent, and the last trips were slow and painful. My arms felt as if they were being pulled out of the sockets as I lugged a heavy keg of nails to finish the tool shed."[127]

Resting on the rock pile, Elmer began thinking about the sacks of cement and sand that would also have to be carried up for the foundation and walls. They needed a real road up the hill to allow horse-drawn delivery trucks to reach the job site.

That evening he placed a few calls to some local people, and the very next morning a George Hartman showed up with a wagon drawn by a stout pair of horses. George and Elmer looked the situation over and discovered the traces of an old road up to two giant willows on the other side of a tumbling brook. They decided if they could bridge the brook, the old road would be usable. They walked up the route to its end at the quarry cliff. Hartman thought they could cut the bank, let the road turn north to the building site, and then do some scraping and filling to make a passable road. So while Hartman scraped and dumped and scraped and filled, Elmer and friends deepened the lower channel for the stream and ordered several lengths of 18' tile pipe to carry the water, covered the pipe with branches, and then topped those with old logs. Protected by some sod, this base for the dirt being dumped from the hillside above bridged the brook and connected the new road with the driveway.[128]

Hartman suggested laying up a wall where the driveway met River Road and filling it in with dirt to street level, making a flatter entrance. Elmer used a sawed off section of a small oak tree to tamp the extra dirt down solidly. Cinders from the local paper mill not only covered and hardened the road surface but also prevented weeds from growing.

Once the road was completed, the shed was finished in only two days. Even with the road, it was still a problem getting materials to the building site. It took four trips for the horse-drawn wagon to get all the cement to the top of the hill, and then there was the sand and the gravel. Once unloaded, the materials took up most of the area.

Elmer began mixing the concrete for the foundation forms. A big Swiss day laborer came by just in time to help Elmer mix the concrete by hand and dump it into the forms for the foundation. The job was finished on 7 September, Elmer's birthday. They mixed more cement for hydro proofing the foundation walls. They were finished just before an early cold snap froze everything, including all the dahlia bulbs stored in the tool house. The early winter halted all building operations.

The following March (1925), Elmer started building again. He hired a laborer to help dig ditches and cut up fallen trees. Pouring the foundation had shown that water was needed near the job site, so Elmer ordered a ram pump to move the water uphill. He and Berta talked about piping the overflow spillage from the pump house down to the stream at the base of the hill. Then they decided a waterfall would be much more attractive.

Below the quarry wall the ground was swampy. Digging revealed a brick wall. After shoveling out water soaked leaves and mud, they found a circular brick reservoir that had once caught water from the springhouse above. It could easily become a pool at the base of the waterfall.

In the evenings Berta and Elmer drew plans for their waterfall. It would have a series of catch basins and trenches for the water flowing down the hill. Berta now had some time to spend at the site, and thoroughly enjoyed working on something permanent instead of repetitive housework. On weekends Elmer and friends gathered stones from the hillside in buckets to make the catch basins. Berta gathered these into piles, wheel barrowing them to the worksite. Toby Carroll and Lem Parton used stone hammers to break up the largest ones, and everyone worked on mixing the mortar and laying up the stones.

As they worked their way uphill the rain-soaked earth would start sliding under their feet, and then the stream would wash the land away. Berta suggested catching the stream higher up where it spilled from the springhouse and building a flume to carry it over their heads. Her plan worked, and the waterfall began to take shape.

Elmer worked alone on the waterway during the week. He figured using fewer but larger stones would save time. But one morning a large stone he was wrestling slipped in his wet gloves and pinned his right hand to the wall of the runway. It was too early for anyone to be about, and he was frightened. He knew he'd be stuck there until Berta came looking for him—and that could be a long time.

He said later he "broke the silence of the morning with some pretty strong cursing," but that did nothing but let off steam. It was up to him to figure things out. He kept moving his free hand around the stone until he eventually managed to get his left hand under the stone and lift it up into position. That finally freed his right hand, and he was able to move. Fortunately, the hand was not broken—just bruised. Still, work was held up for several days while it healed.

Once finished with the hill work, they started mixing the concrete for the pump slab. It required using a block and fall, as well as considerable heaving and pushing to get the pump on its slab. The laborer dug a trench from the site up to the foundation wall where Elmer had left an opening for a drive pipe—the water would first be used in the house before going up to another reservoir at the highest point of the property.

Laying stone for the pump house went quickly and proved to be valuable practice for constructing the stone walls of the house. George Hartman brought his team of horses back with equipment to dig the hole for the hill reservoir. Another pipe then brought water back down the hill to the pump house, the waterfall performed as planned, and everyone admired it. It could be seen from the road, and the twinkling waters became the notable feature of what was now called "Willow Hill."

By June they were ready to start on the house and decided to build the central fireplace first. One of the information pamphlets put out by the government suggested ducts under the floor could conduct air heated in the back of the fireplace into the rest of the house. That seemed like a useful idea. Friend and architect Ross Pfhol explained the principle of the cantilever and gave advice on constructing the slab to support the hood. They designed the wide fireplace with no sides so heat could pour everywhere into the room. Firebricks from an old dye factory edged the slab, and they used fieldstone of all sizes and colors for the fireplace itself. A local blacksmith made the damper—10-feet wide and 60-feet long—operated by an iron rod on one side. They planned holes for adding more pipes and flues later, since they'd learned it was difficult to cut through a finished stone wall.

They built the hood and continued the wall up to where the chimney would start. By mid-June they were able to remove the form at the top of the hood and kindle a small fire on the hearth. A steady stream of smoke poured out of the upper opening. Success!

Now they had to build the upper floor, which would be supported by two twenty-six foot long girders, each fourteen inches square, and twenty-one cross beams. The local mill owner said he could supply the girders and beams at a reasonable cost, but the wood would be green. Since the Haders figured the early settlers must have used green wood—there wouldn't have been time to let it dry—they could use it as well. The mill man noted that oak beams that heavy would need supports, but if they used the lighter and stronger tulip poplar the room could be open. They chose the poplar.

They needed more help to get the roof on and the house closed up before winter. Inside work could be done later. Going over their accounts, they decided they were able to hire some stone masons and a man to carry stone for the needed number of days. Asking around for recommendations, the only affordable helpers were John and Rocco—the same ones who had built the unusable chimney for the garage fireplace. Elmer knew their constructive ideas were apt to go haywire, and they would need more direction to make sure they followed Elmer's plans, not their own ideas.

Since no one started their work before eight, Elmer had time to set up for the day's work. John and Rocco were often puzzled by his ideas, such as having hinges built into the walls to support the doors and windows. They usually went along with Elmer's unorthodox suggestions but often chose to do things the way they always had. Elmer preferred the look of larger stones in a wall, but his helpers frequently broke up the big ones since the smaller ones were easier to lift. They filled in the holes in the walls that Elmer had left for future pipes, or used the nicest stones on walls that would be plastered over. They needed constant supervision.

Elmer started to worry about running short of stone, so he ordered brick and hollow tiles to fill in. These could be set up much faster. John and Rocco didn't like the tile and took as much time to grout it as they did the stone. However, the weather cleared, and the walls reached seven feet. After the men quit work for the day, Elmer and Berta raised the scaffolding, built forms for the concrete lintels or prepared the wood ones to go over doors. At dusk they too called it a day, walked home to Lyall Cottage, and took a hot shower or a dip in the Hudson.

Toby Carroll and his mother, Hamilton Williamson, were visiting when the girders and beams arrived. When she saw how huge they were, she gave Elmer seventy-five dollars to hire someone else to put them in place. Elmer hired a man named Johnson for thirty dollars. A week of rain stalled the project, but finally they heard a noisy Model T chugging up the road. Five children, ages nine to fifteen tumbled out of the back. Johnson was the strongest man any of them had ever seen, able to lift a green twenty-six foot long timber while the Haders wrapped chains around it. When he hitched his block and fall to a girder, Berta, Elmer, and all five children pulled, while Johnson shoved and lifted it through the door and into place. By eight o'clock that night the last lintel was in position, and the Johnsons left to a chorus of hurrahs from everyone watching.

Elmer's writer friend, Bob Hyde, was building a house at nearby Palisades, and they decided to swap any unusual tools they might need. Since Bob had a chain hoist, he came over and they used it to put the beams in place. The Haders would hire carpenters later to put up the rafters, also heavy because of being green lumber.

Berta and Elmer painted everything likely to be embedded in cement, as well as all the raw ends and tops of the beams. Those were also covered with tarpaper. The damp weather continued, but they worked on the rear walls. With the weekenders' help, they cleared a spot for the future studio addition to the house. When a huge chestnut stump blocked the way, they just left it in the ground and built over it.

As the stone walls were going up, the Haders decided to build niches for tiny plants into the walls along with recesses for birds. These little bird houses had hinges for doors, and little balconies for the birds to rest on. That was one innovative idea that appealed to mason John so he made one too. He brought sea shells from home, studded them like stars in the concrete, and cemented a larger shell to the stone that served as perch. There were nineteen bird houses when the house was finally finished, and other little niches for flowers.

The days were getting shorter. The work needed to speed up. Elmer got up in the dark, and worked with Berta in the rain after the men went home. A laborer was hired to make the wet concrete while they worked on the inside fireplace, putting a large flat stone they had saved in the center of the hood where the chimney started. They rigged up pulleys on each side of fireplace to lift the stone and cement. Once the flue lining and chimney were finished, Rocco cemented in a ten cent piece, and John wired a horseshoe on for good luck.

The walls were finished by mid-August. Though the house couldn't yet be seen from the road, neighbors were beginning to show up and admire the house, which looked larger than it really was. After listening to Elmer talk about how so many garages blocked the views of the river and why they were attempting to save as many trees as possible, they invited him to join Grand View's village zoning board in 1926. Elmer, now considered by his neighbors to be "a knowledgeable builder," was chosen to be its first administrator. His "passion to keep Grand View small, beautiful, and green" kept him in the same office for 44 years—and he served without compensation or expenses.[129]

They decided to use hollow tile wherever main electrical wires entered the house, as well as for any additions. These could be faced with stone later. The tile went up quickly, especially since Berta discovered she was good at setting it up. Soon she had the studio walls up to five feet, and later built the west wall entirely by herself. When her brother Godfrey came to visit from teaching at

Cornell University, he was not only impressed with the house but especially with his sister's achievement.

When they found cheap lumber could be had from old ice-houses being torn down, they ordered enough to cover the main roof. Though dry, the old ice house beams had to be cut and fit separately too—the angles in the roof valley were difficult to figure out. A 3x6 piece that had curved up at each end became an "interesting ridge." By autumn the house was completely under roof, and indoor work could begin.

A friend, Henry Poor, had recently built a house and discovered that stone floors were cold. He suggested covering them with chestnut boards, much less expensive than oak. The local supplied the tongue and grooved boards. At the end of September a large group of weekenders—the Partons, Eve Chappel, Hamilton Williamson, Toby Carroll, John Gregg, along with Bessie and her new friend, British actor Bill Sauter—stacked and slatted all the boards. On later weekends they laid the two inch thick chestnut flooring and worked on some of the other indoor jobs. Elmer used extra chestnut boards to build a huge table that could seat thirty to forty people. The money saved from Hamilton Williamson's girder gift for installing the beams was enough for the dining room chairs.

It was still only a big shell of a house but it was complete enough for thirty-two of their friends to come to the housewarming annual Thanksgiving get together. Since everyone had helped build it, stone by stone, they all enjoyed seeing the final results. Miska Petersham showed Elmer how to build a good log fire, and soon six-foot logs were roaring in the fireplace. Still, the house was so cold that the guests kept their coats on. They turned a turkey in a spit in the great fireplace, and used another fireplace to boil the potatoes and turnips.[130] As usual, everybody brought something to the feast. It was another great meal with interesting friends, and the little stone house was on its way to becoming "Hader Heaven," a welcoming home for all.

As *Asia* Editor, Elsie Weil put it in her post-Thanksgiving thank-you letter:

> The turkey's hump is a lovely lump
> Which you cannot see at the Zoo;
> But lovelier yet is the hump that we get
> From eating Thanksgiving, too.
>
> Gertrude and Elsie too-oo-oo
> When we eat too much of the goo-oo-oo
> We get the hump—
> Turkeelious hump—
> The hump that doubles in two.
>
> And there ought to be a corner for me
> (As well as the thirty-and two)
> When we get the hump—
> Turkeelious hump—
> The hump that doubles in two.
>
> The cure for this ill is not to sit still,
> Or frowst[131] by the Haders' new fire;
> But to take a large pail and a hammer and nail,
> And knock till we gently perspire.
>
> We'll get it—the thirty and two-oo-oo
> If we haven't enough to do-oo-oo,
> We'll all get the hump—
> Turkeelious hump—
> Every-one of the thirty and two.[132]

CHAPTER SIX

BRANCHING PATHS:
MAGAZINES TO BOOKS

Berta and Elmer had achieved their major goal—they were now living in a house of their own on a hill with a view similar to the old studio on Telegraph Hill. The studio was planned after the one Elmer had had in Paris, but was lit by a tall north-facing window. Elmer and Berta usually did their illustrating on the platform which became a stage for the plays often put on by the weekenders. Their friends continued to come, bringing new friends and bearing gifts of food and presents for the house. Mary Margaret talked of Berta being "pretty as a picture" in the peasant dresses she liked to wear, with her curly hair controlled by a cap or kerchief. The Kemps remember that she wore neutral colors in public, but "at home she bloomed into lovely peasant colors, brilliant head scarves, skirts full and to the ankle, . . . and an embroidered over-apron. Her blouses were usually white guimpes gathered at the neck with black velvet ribbon."[133]

Jane Barrow remembers the Haders as "always being 'centered down,' concerned with zoning, ecology, birth control, with pure intentions toward the world. And surrounded by galaxies of ambitious, gifted, struggling, contentious, often bitter people who came to them for comfort and fun."[134] Elmer enjoyed playing the guitar, and the group often had good times making music and putting on skits. The studio, raised above the main floor like a stage, had curtains that could be pulled to hide the mess inside.

Rose Wilder Lane had recently filed suit against Frederick O'Brien for the royalties she was owed—with a best seller, they should have been substantial. Since she had lost the original contract and had nothing to show he had signed it, he refused to pay her a thing. Now she accused Berta of losing a hatbox in which Rose thought she'd hidden her contract.[135] Berta managed to calm her down and their friendship continued.

The Thanksgiving feasts continued as a yearly tradition. Christmas gatherings brought friends and strangers to spend Christmases at Willow Hill. These were rich with the warmth of friendships, good conversations, and the smell of good things to eat emanating from the kitchen.

But the Haders needed income. Even as they celebrated the completion of their new home at Thanksgiving, they were learning that their major source of income—magazine illustration—was disappearing. *Metropolitan Magazine*, an excellent market for Elmer's cover illustrations, had just ceased publication due to changes in ownership.

And now the U.S. Post Office was cracking down on children's pages in the magazines sent by second-class mail. This rate applied only to the editorial content of the magazines: the advertising portion was assessed at a higher rate. Apparently "advertisers and others tried to sneak non-magazine content into magazines so they could send them at the low second-class mailing rate. Now the post office was scrutinizing magazine content, and the children's pages did not seem editorial in nature. Ergo: if a serious magazine contained them, it had to be mailed at a more expensive rate.[136] Naturally, the magazines dropped the pages. No more of those delightful projects that kept children busy while their parents read the editorial content in peace and quiet. And no more dependable income to support the little stone house.

Many people speculated that the loss of their only child spurred their interest in children's writing, but they were already doing that kind of work when Hammie died. They enjoyed children! They welcomed them into their home and enjoyed watching them play around Willow Hill. Children sometimes built dams in the stream. Two little neighborhood girls offered to buy the ravine by the house for ten cents, but the Haders politely declined. Nevertheless the girls continued to go to the property on "secret missions" and climb up the twinkling springs to elude their brothers. They usually didn't get wet but were often scolded for sliding down the garage roof where they had their "Main Spy Headquarters."[137]

Children's work was what had paid their living expenses. Their budget was still tight, even without rent. While trying to figure out another source of income, they decided to use their house as collateral for a thousand dollar loan from the local bank. The bank responded that "After prayerful consideration" they felt that "while the architectural style of their house probably suited them, it didn't qualify as a very sound investment."[138] However, they were willing to loan them five hundred dollars. That would help.

Where else to turn? Mary Margaret McBride had recently met Alexander Williams, a public relations man who oozed charm, and the two had bantered about what charm really was. Alex suggested they write a book about it, and now *Charm: A Book About Those Who Have It And Those Who Want It* was going to be published by the Rae D. Henkle publishing company. (The book was a spoof, and they were all quite surprised when it was actually used as a textbook in some secondary schools.[139]) Elmer was a mutual friend of both, so he was asked to design the jacket and provide some illustrations. The company not only accepted his designs but also hired him to illustrate a forthcoming book on math concepts for children. Elmer's bright illustrations enhanced and explained *Donald in Numberland*, and educational texts gave him another possible avenue for the Hader creativity.

Friend and illustrator Willy Pogany, who had also created magazine covers for the defunct *Metropolitan Magazine,* had formerly illustrated many books of fairy tales and myths in England and America. Now he was illustrating them again. Due to his encouragement other friends like Miska and Maude Petersham had also entered the field. The Petershams had received enough illustration commissions to enable them to buy a house near an artist colony in Woodstock, a couple of hours from Grand View.[140] The Haders realized that children's books were not only a growing field, but also much longer-lived than magazines. Royalties kept coming in as long as the book stayed in print, instead of a single payment for a magazine piece.

Children's book departments were just beginning to be established in publishing houses. Libraries had focused on children since the beginning of the twentieth century, but publishers had ignored the market. They relied on imports and reprints from the classics. Even as the genre was developing, author Frank Baum had to share costs for his original *The Wizard of Oz* with the publisher, including paying for the cost of the plates.[141]

Before the First World War, British and American working class youth read the cheap and sensational "penny dreadfuls" printed on pulp paper and easily available. Edward Stratemeyer capitalized on the craze for serials that had become popular for children in the 1800s, ranging from *Peck's Bad Boys* by George Peck to books by Louisa May Alcott and Henry Alger. Like Alger, Stratemeyer founded his own syndicate, similar to those in newspapers, hiring available writers to work on plot outlines developed by the syndicate. They created series like the *Rover Boys* and *Bobbsey Twins* for a variety of different publishers.

Franklin K. Mathiews, librarian of the Boy Scouts of America, did not approve of these reading materials. He began urging booksellers in 1913 to encourage moral development in young people by producing books with higher standards. In 1916, the Boston Women's Educational and Industrial Union had established a small children's bookstore under the guidance of Bertha E. Mahoney. She complained that although Europe produced glorious picture books, America did not, because publishers did not make children's books "the responsibility of *one* able person."[142] Mahoney also sold adult titles, including the first Crossword Puzzle Book and was delighted to find that, too, spurred children's self-directed learning.

When the Great War ended in 1918, everyone expected the world to become a better place. America looked forward to future world leadership. In 1919, President Wilson took time out from working on the League of Nations to proclaim the week of 8 June as National Boy Scout Week. Mathiews made another speech to the American Booksellers Association (ABA), pointing out that publishers had recently been making and selling books for the four million soldiers under arms—but ignoring the ten million boys between ages ten and sixteen who also needed good books to read. That was a marketing argument publishers could understand. It may have given a reason for George P. Brett, Sr., chairman of Macmillan Company of New York, to create the Department of Books for Boys and Girls. Macmillan had experience in children's books since they imported many from their headquarters in London.

After an abortive experience with a male editor, Brett had the acumen to replace him with Louise Seaman, one of his staff. A recent Vassar graduate, she had taught for three years in a private progressive school in Boston before finally achieving her dream of working in the field of publishing. (When she'd been appointed editor of the Vassar newspaper, the college president told her she could never expect a career in literature without courses in French and German, even though she was already fluent in the languages.[143])

Mathiews' speech certainly inspired Frederic Melcher, the young co-editor of *Publishers Weekly,* to persuade the ABA to sponsor a Children's Book Week. He and Mathiews worked with Anne Carroll Moore, New York Public Library's children's librarian, to plan the festivities. They also invited Louise Seaman to help. Popular artist Jessie Wilcox Smith did the banner, promoting "More Books in the Home."

Seaman did such a good job with her first list that Doubleday followed by hiring May Massee, another gifted young woman. Publishing had long been the domain of gentlemen only, but it was generally believed that "women knew more than men about children, and were thus better-equipped for work that ministered to children's needs."[144] These young women studied literature in college, and had high standards for what they chose to publish. Their books did well: other American publishers began to develop their own departments.

Children's rooms in libraries were becoming well-established, led by the redoubtable Anne Carroll Moore of the New York Public Library. As more children's librarians entered the scene, also with backgrounds in literature, they shared opinions about the best books in library journals and at conferences. Children's book reviews began appearing in the major newspapers and review journals. Parents in the 1920s saw education—and books—as a key to America's future and appreciated their recommendations.

Department stores now sold books along with clothes and household goods. During the 1920s they often had salespeople called "Readers' Advisors" to help adults choose books they would enjoy. These advisors also promoted good children's books. In 1922, Frederic Melcher created an award to recognize the best children's book of the year. The award was to be called the Newbery Medal, named after early children's publisher, John Newbery. The American Library Association approved his idea, and established a committee of children's librarians to choose these quality children's books. Each prize-winning publisher received gold medal stickers to place on the book's jackets, which informed purchaser and the salesperson that the particular book was outstanding.

Berta and Elmer read those newspaper reviews of new children's books with interest. They talked it over and decided to see what the possibilities were. Maybe some of their magazine work could be made into books. Certainly the Mother Goose illustrations from the *Christian Science Monitor* and *Good Housekeeping* would be perfect for a new edition of the classic. They took their portfolio into New York to show to some of these new editors: Virginia Kirkus, May Massee, and Louise Seaman.

Their timing was perfect for Macmillan since Louise Seaman was looking for new artists. Charles Stringer of the Jersey City Printing Company had developed some new color printing techniques for creating small inexpensive books, and Seaman realized these would meet a market need. She'd decided to create a series of newly illustrated children's stories. Even though the format might be cheap, she still wanted excellence and decided to have a contest for new artists who could work within the printer's guidelines. Once she saw the Haders' work, she invited them to enter. As Louise Seaman wrote later, "The dummy for *The Ugly Duckling* done by the Haders stood out above all the rest of the artists' samples. It was so simple, so childish, so funny; the ducks were well-drawn; the layout was artistic without being 'arty'; the heavy black line meant a keyplate which would live and a definite rhythm for the eye of a young person."[145] They received contracts for four of the Happy Hour books and immediately set to work.

They managed to give a variety of color effects that added to the story's atmosphere, even though limited by the black and three-color printing process. Elmer had learned much of this from his impressionist studies in France, where they studied Chevreul's theory of how colors appeared more intensive when placed next to other complementary colors.[146]

As Louise Seaman explained, "At the time when they first started, many publishers limited artists based on the expense of reproducing color and half-tone artwork, particularly in the genre of picture books. What I appreciate about the Haders' early work is the way they worked masterfully within those limits."[147] They were extremely lucky to start this new career under the tutelage of Louise Seaman. Her mother and sister were both artists and she understood the graphics of book production. Eunice Blake, an assistant to Seaman and later an editor in her own right, said Louise brought the same enthusiasm to her editing as she had to her teaching. "She always expected more of her authors and her employees than they thought they had in them, and usually brought out abilities that one did not know one had."[148]

Besides being easy to work with, the Haders were fun to have around. The entire department was enthralled with the sketches embellishing their correspondence. Elmer was always shown with an exaggerated nose, and Berta with extremely curly hair. These features continued in any illustration that included themselves. One sketch showed them in their office hard at work on the pictures, and another showed Elmer delivering the manuscripts in a wagon drawn by *Chicken Little and the Little Half Chick*.[149]

Fortunately, their house was livable if not finished, and they were used to working long hours when needed. They got right to work on sketches for the Happy Hour books, and Elmer also completed a contract for a jacket for *Stronghold* by Burke Boyce from Viking Press. He followed through with the illustrations for Mary Margaret McBride's *Charm* and Jean Peedie's *Donald in Numberland* for Henkle Publishing and turned those in as well. Those books came out swiftly. Since the Happy Hour series was new, producing both text and pictures in a format that satisfied both Louise Seaman and the Haders took time.

By the end of 1927 they had produced six books and their new book career was officially launched. Their friends teased them about turning out a book a month. That may have reminded Elmer of his "A Sketch A Minute" vaudeville act, because he sent Macmillan a picture with two sketches of himself: as a statue with a harp in front of a 1912 audience, and then in 1927 as a statue holding up *The Ugly Duckling* book at a book signing in the Abraham Strauss department store's book department.

When Cornelia Meigs sent in the completed manuscript for *The Wonderful Locomotive*, Seaman needed an illustrator who could draw for small boys and who knew all about steam engines. Much to her surprise she discovered Elmer to be the son of a railroad man, who had also worked on a locomotive after the San Francisco fire. He was also good friends with the men who worked at the local roundhouse. Berta reportedly loved Meigs' story, they got the job, and visitors to the house reported that "both of them smile when it is mentioned and I heard Elmer chuckling out loud while he worked on it."[150]

Even though Elmer and Berta turned out far more illustrations than she needed for *The Wonderful Locomotive,* Seaman couldn't turn down a single one. "Who could leave out one of them—the faces of the brakeman and engineers in the lantern light, the boy and dog peering out of the cab window . . . pennies must be counted again and every picture fitted into its perfect place."[151] Cornelia Meigs was equally delighted. Even within the confines of printing guidelines, the Haders were able to convey their humor, humanity, and attention to precise details.

They didn't know it then, but they were embarking on a lifelong award-winning career. The royalties were split fifty-fifty between author and illustrator. As usual, the Haders split their share equally between them. Both Berta and Elmer were used to earning separate paychecks for their art, and when they shared their "thought sketches" to be combined into the completed art, it seemed natural to ask Macmillan to send each of them their own check. A 1972 Interoffice Memo from one of the Macmillan people noted, however, that Women's Lib had not caught up with the Royalty Department—Elmer always got the odd penny.[152] After all, many of their friends were suffragists, and talk about the rights of women was frequent table conversation.

The success of *The Wonderful Locomotive* and the Happy Hour books firmly established the Haders in their field. Berta and Elmer understood the art of printing well enough to create drawings that worked for the printer, and they became known for their wonderful use of color. Three more Happy Hour books arrived on the market in 1928 from Macmillan, along with a book published by E. P. Dutton, Emerson's *Adventures of Theodore Roosevelt*, illustrated solely by Elmer. Hamilton Williamson wrote the text for one of Frank Buck's stories, *A Monkey's Tale*, and asked the Haders to illustrate it. Several publishers rejected that one, but it amused May Massie at Doubleday.[153] Both of them worked on *The Picture Book of Travel,* showing samples of life through the ages. This was another book whose colorful illustrations taxed the printing process. Elmer visited the printers often to get the effects he wanted.

The 1929 productions included educational books that Elmer illustrated for Harper & Brothers: *The Story of Water Supply* and *The Story of Markets* by Ruth Orton Camp, Hamilton Williamson's *A Monkey Tale*, and a French tale, *The Story of Mr. Punch* by Octave Feuillet. The Haders had great fun doing the silhouettes for their own creation, *Two Funny Clowns.*

They took editorial suggestions seriously and usually settled differences in an amiable fashion. When a 1929 letter from Coward McCann suggested, "The clown illustrations are wonderful, but . . . some kind of measured rhythm in the compact easily read light couplets might do it," the Haders replied: "The decision as to whether it shall be all jingle or a jinglet now and then I will leave to you. Louise Seaman is not terribly keen on jingles. May Massee does not think they are so hot. Virginia Kirkus is not for them. On the other hand Bertha Gunterman at Longman, Green & Co. likes them. Dutton ditto. Personally I think a couplet now and then would be the thing."[154] Longman did like verses: they published *What'll You Do When You Grow Up?* entirely in rhymes.

Two Funny Clowns wound up with no rhymes, but the jacket flap stated it "was written with an artful lilt—the parent who has to read it aloud will be pleased." The book hardly needed words. The black silhouettes of the characters had enough humor and action to stand by themselves. However, the next year Berta and Elmer wrote another rhyming text for Bertha Gunterman: *Lions and Tigers and Elephants Too.* They'd learned that getting jobs meant meeting editorial desires.

Children's departments were bringing in good profits. The backlists were a profitable segment for publishers since upfront costs had already been paid; bookstores were delighted to recommend and reorder favorites, and children's worn-out library books needed frequent replacing. The adult Literary Guild—a popular source for mail order books—spun off a book club for children, called the Junior Literary Guild. An author could expect royalties for a published book to keep coming for years.

No one foresaw the stock market crash. Few realized the impact it would have on the publishing business.

✦ CHAPTER SEVEN ✦

EDITORS, PUBLISHERS, AND BRIDGE WARS

By the end of the 1920s, Berta and Elmer's new career was well-launched. Their former schedules stayed in place for illustrating, writing, working on the house and gardens, and weekend entertaining. Berta, reluctant to leave Willow Hill, let Elmer make most of the trips into the city. When there, Elmer spent time at the various printers to see what was new in inks and technology and to make sure they were communicating well.

The 1929 stock market crash was stunning but at first it affected only those who had sums of money invested.[155] It had little immediate impact on the Haders' lives since they had no investments, no debts, and were used to living on what they earned. Since childhood both Berta and Elmer had been exposed to Ben Franklin's famous ditty:

Use it up,
Wear it out,
Make it do, or
Do without.

This was the way they always had lived. They used the backs of envelopes, letters, and advertisements as notepaper. Elmer had a knack for rolling old newspapers into logs for the fireplace. The few loans they took out from friends or the local bank were always paid back as soon as possible. They did break down and spend five dollars on a Weber grand piano someone had for sale. This investment added a wonderful dimension to the entertainment on the Hader weekends. It sat in a corner, facing Elmer's early painting of Berta, and the snapshots of Elmer at the piano look as if he is playing directly to her portrait. A sketch of it was sent in a letter to Louise, showing they could now join the musical weekends offered by Louise and her new husband, Edwin de Turck Bechtel.

Macmillan continued to be their main publisher. Louise, a thorough editor, was always positive, even when sending them three or more pages of corrections and/or changes, such as those for *The Farmer in The Dell.* She noted that dell meant a small valley and "the end papers make the farm look too flat for a dell." She continued editing, line by line: "Poplar trees are too short-lived to be by the farmhouse—use maples." "You don't stack hay until it is dry." "Go find a blacksmith shop and watch what happens. I am certain this picture is wrong." Just before the book was to be published, Elmer had his own correction to make. One of the weekend houseguests mentioned a fuss in California about a billboard displaying a young mother without a marriage ring. The Haders suddenly realized they had forgotten to include one for the farmer's wife "and wouldn't have the younger generation think that the farmer's wife was living in sin. Would Macmillan send them all drawings in which the farmer's wife (sic) left hand would expose her apparent guilt?" Friend Guy Moyston, now living in New York, could pick them up and bring them out to the Haders to put on the ring—unless Macmillan was willing to accept the idea of common-law marriage.[156] The missing ring was added.

Even Seaman didn't always accept their various ideas for books. Working on the Mother Goose rhymes had given Elmer the idea of writing a story of Humpty Dumpty before his "mishap." She apparently didn't think much of that idea, so it remained in the files for possible future use. They kept busy illustrating the animal stories by their old friend Hamilton Williamson, and were delighted when Coward McCann accepted their edition of Mother Goose.[157] They didn't like the first results, however—Elmer thought the printing, particularly of "Twinkle Twinkle Little Star" looked "cheap." But after Charles Stringer reprinted everything, producing a lively and colorful edition, Elmer was satisfied with the changes made— though he still asked Stringer to send the preliminary proofs.[158]

Editors usually found the Haders easy to work with—besides Louise Seaman at Macmillan, they created books and illustrations for May Massee of the Doubleday juvenile department, Bertha L. Gunterman at Longman, Green & Co., Marion Fiery at Alfred A. Knopf, and Virginia Kirkus at Harper & Brothers. Children's departments were still small, and the editors, writers, and artists all knew one another. They could and did keep up with each other's new publications as they came out.

In the 1920s new books seemed exciting to the parents and children, as well as librarians. Writers and illustrators met and talked to customers at the book departments in large stores, such as

Marshall Fields in Chicago, Hudson's in Detroit, and Halle Brothers in Cleveland.[159] Bertha Gunterman was delighted to hear the results of one Hader visit to the Chicago Public Library arranged by the publisher. They'd showed their work and talked about their pictures to "between five and six hundred children." The librarian reported, "They are the most delightful people I have ever had the pleasure of meeting and their pictures . . . reflect even more the interest and delight which I know they take in the children."[160] Good publicity.

According to a 1949 article by editor Rose Dobbs, almost every book they wrote had a particular reader in mind. "*Spunky* is 'a pony for Louise.' *Green and Gold* was made for 'the banana planter's bride,' and *The Little Stone House* is a 'surprise for Leota.'"[161] Rose also referred to the cameos on the dedication pages that "present a rare tongue-in-cheek thumbnail autobiography." All of these helped the Haders' personality shine through.[162]

The Haders were also willing to listen to editorial advice, knowing these editors were working with them to produce better books. *Spunky* was based on Elmer's childhood memory about writing to Santa every year for a little white pony.[163] Seaman was enthusiastic about the information about the background and the various uses of Shetland ponies in *Spunky*, but thought it too lengthy for a two dollar book. She sent a letter outlining places to cut and suggested she could find someone else to do the selecting and revision of the text while the Haders worked on the pictures.

The Haders often differed with editors and readers—but their sense of humor often left all sides happy. Marion Fiery at Alfred A. Knopf issued *Under the Pignut Tree*, the first book of a planned series of four seasonal stories. In mid-April 1930 she wrote to Berta and Elmer enclosing a letter she'd received from a Mr. V. M. Schenck of a Springfield, Massachusetts, bindery.

> We note that there is to be a series of four, the scenes to be laid in Spring supposed to be related to Spring. In this, it seems to us that you are making a mistake, since grasshoppers seldom appear until the warm days of August; crickets, likewise, are seldom heard until the last of August or early September, Summer, Fall, and Winter respectively.
>
> Under the circumstances, it would seem much better to label this book as the "Summer" item. Perhaps the authors have already thought of this, but we feel quite sure that this inconsistency will occur to a good many readers, and if we are to teach children the love of nature through books, they must be essentially true to fact.[164]

In a handwritten postscript Fiery asked, "What shall I say to him? Everyone here thinks the books look swell!"[165]

Apparently Elmer and Berta decided the answer was to show, not tell. Willow Hill had plenty of grasshoppers. They picked a good-sized one, put him in a cotton-lined box with leaves and grass and sent the box in to Knopf. On 29 April Fiery sent the Haders a letter saying that "Little Elmer brought youth and life and spring to the office all day, as well as verification. He has just departed on his next journey to Mr. Schenck, c/o the Huntting Company, at Springfield, Mass. We all join in hoping that Elmer will have enough energy left after the trip to leap up and scare him."[166]

The mail service must have been fast, for on "Mayday" her memo contained a copy of Mr. Schenk's 30 April reply:

Dear Miss Fiery:

'Elmer' arrived this morning, seemingly happy and content—with the structure of a grasshopper but "as lively as a cricket." Of course when I talked about grasshoppers I had a full-grown New England grasshopper in mind, not the puny hot-house variety such as artists breed for models. 'Elmer' hardly looks as if he could carry an elf on his back, though not having been on intimate terms with an elf for many years, I had almost forgot just how weighty they are.

Had it occurred to you that it might be a good plan to offer a live grasshopper with every copy of the book; this would mean a particularly strong sale in the early spring when grasshoppers are rare birds. No charge for this suggestion, though in event of its resulting in an enormous sale of the book, I would not mind sharing the royalties.

Seriously, I do appreciate the thoroughness with which the Haders defend their book and gracefully retire from the field 'a vanquished critic.'[167]

Elmer said later that the grasshopper was not puny when he was packed. The journey must have been hard on him.

When a promised manuscript was late, the Haders wrote a funny sixteen page book, *All's Well That Ends Well*,[168] showing how "Mr. Flumonia" had attacked Elmer while he was working, and Berta had spent all her time nursing him back to health. With a gift of such an illustrated book, how could Louise not forgive?

The worsening economy eventually impacted the publishing business. After George Brett, Sr., the founder of Macmillan's children's department, decided to retire in 1931, his son, George, Jr., took over. He was not the fan of children's books that his father had been. He told Seaman she could no longer offer a contract until all the costs were submitted ahead of time. Expense accounts were called for. When the Haders submitted their expense account for a 1931 New Haven American Library Association meeting, Seaman must have chuckled. Each item—from taxis, to porters, to the electrician at the hall is pictured on the list, along with the cost. The expenses for the trip to New Haven, Connecticut, totaled $15.25— much of it given in tips.[169]

Contracts with publishers were beginning to slow down. The Editorial Committee of the Publisher's Association decided to make contracts on the basis of net wholesale price instead of list. The royalty of 15% wholesale sounded better than 10% of the list price but was actually a financial cut.[170]

In 1931 Berta and Elmer had published three books including illustrating two by old friend Hamilton Williamson. Even with the cutbacks in late 1932, and a rejection by Scribner's of a manuscript that later became *The Mighty Hunter*, the Haders wrote optimistically that they were sure "All those interested in better books for children, and by this we mean parents, teachers, librarians, and booksellers, as well as the writers, artists, editors and publishers, will find a way to insure a steady and continuous supply."[171] An attempt to try *Good Housekeeping,* once a strong market for the Haders, received a very terse rejection: "The reader's report on your *Fly-Away Plane* is, in effect, thumbs down. Sorry. I suppose you want us to hold it until you call."[172]

However, Elmer continued his weekly city visits and talked to the editorial departments at the various publishing houses. Whenever he heard of a possible assignment, the Haders would brainstorm together to generate ideas. Interested and capable editors helped them turn their ideas and dummies into published books and often suggested sources for research.

The Haders strove for accuracy in every detail. Usually they began by reading what was available, researching in libraries, and by writing to any government department that might have information on the topic. The California Fish and Game department helped their proposed *Cedric the Seal* become *Tooky, The Story of a Seal Who Joined the Circus*. When Harper & Brothers accepted the idea for *Berta and Elmer Hader's Picture Book of the States*, Kirkus suggested that besides relying on material sent by the state's visitor centers, they might also use the *Blue Books* put out every year or so by each state. These contained current descriptions of the state including its resources, commerce, and government.

The Haders came up with colorful maps for 26 states, showing their inhabitants farming or fishing, working and playing, against bright backgrounds of a blooming land. These were carefully designed to fit into the 48 pages allocated to the book. Each map also showed some of the famous historical figures along with the modern ones, and each had Berta and Elmer peering in to the state from the outside. However, Kirkus said that libraries would be a big buyer and distributor of the proposed book, and they would insist on all 48 states being included. So would the Junior Literary Guild.

Elmer insisted that each map had to have its own page, so forty-eight maps meant forty-eight pages—leaving no room for notes, answers, or commentary. Doing it Elmer's way would cost more than Harper was willing to finance. As a good editor, caring for both manuscript and budget, Kirkus pointed out that they could pair up some neighboring states. Illinois and Indiana, both "skinny" states, could share a page if drawn vertically. So could Vermont and New Hampshire. Oregon and Washington could be stacked on one page. The compromise worked: after much re-working all 48 states were fitted in, along with map index and commentary. Children—and parents—pored over the maps looking for state products, cities, and well-known industries. They also had fun finding bits of state history. Because each state's pictures were distinctive, U.S. geography became much more real.[173]

This disagreement over the number of pages in a book was another indicator of how the Depression was influencing the publishing world. Where Seaman had been willing to fit in more pages than were originally called for by *The Wonderful Locomotive*, editors now had to work within many more constraints. Banks were failing. People were not spending money and also were not having children: the birthrate was dropping. Many publishers felt the children's market was drying up.

The Haders had to work harder to find assignments. Alfred A. Knopf was one of the first to quietly close their children's department.[174] They told Marion Fiery they were closing the children's division and letting Fiery go, just as Berta had convinced her to accept Laura Ingalls Wilder's *Little House in the Big Woods*. Believing it wouldn't get the kind of publication it deserved without a children's department, Fiery sent Rose Wilder Lane a handwritten note suggesting her mother not sign the Knopf contract. She also quietly gave a copy of the book to Virginia Kirkus. The manuscript so enthralled Kirkus that she rode past her train stop, realizing, "Here was a book no Depression could stop."[175] It became an immediate hit, and led to a long-running series. But then in 1932, right after Harper & Brothers published the profitable Wilder book and *Berta and Elmer Hader's Picture Book of the States*, Harper decided to cut their children's department staffing. Rather than agree, Virginia Kirkus left and started her own Kirkus Bookshop Service, promising unbiased views and unerring accuracy. It was successful enough that she never returned to Harper & Brothers.

Doubleday, Doran and Company followed the trend by firing May Massee that fall. This was a huge shock to everyone in the business, since she was widely regarded as a leading editor by librarians and bookstores. Noted librarian Anne Carroll Moore immediately offered her the job of speaker for the Children's Book Week event, and many of the artists Massee had hired remained loyal, promising to stick with her. Soon afterward Viking Press, "a firm with Olympian aspirations," recognized Massee's skills and connections, and hired her on very generous terms to be the founder of Viking Junior Books.

One bit of good news was that Mary Margaret McBride, who'd been out of work as a journalist for several years, now had her own afternoon radio show. She was one of the first radio hosts to realize that though her listeners might be homebound country housewives, they were just as eager as anyone else to find out what was going on in the wider world. She began interviewing as many interesting people of note as she could. She also did her own commercials, only recommending things she had personally used and liked.

Elmer had read an article in a Texas magazine about a movement to rid the plains of the rapidly multiplying herds of burros, an "economic loss" to the state.[176] Berta had memories of the one she'd had when a child of four. Louise Seaman approved the contract, and a letter to the University of Nevada brought much information about burros in the return mail. *Midget and Bridget* begins with the little burros growing up together, and then being separated—one going to the army and one to a poor farmer hard pressed to eke out a living.[177]

Louise Seaman had a major equestrian accident one fall day in 1933. Her horse stumbled and she went flying, breaking her hip when she landed. Since she was laid up for several months to recuperate, George Brett, Jr. let her go, saying it was for health reasons.

It was hard to accept the departure of the other editors with whom the Haders had worked closely, but the loss of Louise Seaman was devastating. They had relied heavily on her advice, abilities, and friendship. However, Brett Junior did have enough sense to retain Seaman's assistant, Doris Patee.

Fortunately, it seems to have been a seamless transition between the two editors. The Haders remained an important part of the Macmillan stable of authors. Louise, her husband Ned Bechtel, and Doris Patee remained close friends through their lifetimes.

Doris Patee was now in charge of *Midget and Bridget,* and she had her own ideas for making the book even better. She apologized to the Haders about her "ruthless" cutting, but she felt it made the story move along more rapidly. Some of the copy had to be cut in order to fit the picture layout, and Patee also increased the leading[178] between the lines to make it easier to read.

Each little burro went off to different adventures, but was reunited at the end of the book. Doris made several suggestions about increasing the tension at their reunion and her suggestions were accepted. Berta included a line about a sweet-voiced woman rescuing the burro, thinking her mother would be thrilled by being mentioned. When Bridget is sold to be a companion for a little girl, the dummy refers to the child as "Berta" though the name didn't appear in the final copy. When Berta later asked Adelaide why she had never commented on the completed book, she was told that, "We never did have a burro." Berta said later maybe it had been a neighbor's burro, but she "had always cherished the belief that it had been theirs."[179]

The book went on to be a children's favorite—who could resist the burros' charming little faces? Susan Hirschman, the editor who took over at Macmillan late in the Hader careers, mentioned how much she'd enjoyed that particular book as a child. The Morris Sanford Company store in Cedar Rapids, Iowa, added two tiny colts named "Midget" and "Bridget" to their Christmas village, where over a thousand children, with parents, came to see them. The store reportedly suggested that teachers in the lower grades might read the book to their children.[180]

The Haders' annual Christmas card featured the burros as well. After using *Tooky* in their 1932 card, rather than the usual Christmas characters, they had repeated the idea with *Spunky*. They enjoyed designing cards around one of their new book characters, and their young relatives loved guessing from the card what book would likely be under their own tree. Berta was an eager reader of the other newly published juveniles, but Elmer rarely read them, saying his aim was freshness and originality and avoidance of even a trace of unintended plagiarism. They both read and loved books about animals, such as *The Wind in the Willows*. Patee encouraged them to continue their own original stories, though she always felt animals were their best subjects. In 1933 they created *Spunky* for Patee, *Chuck-A-Luck and His Reindeer* for Houghton Mifflin, and

Whiffy McMann for Oxford University Press. *Chuck-a-Luck* was based on the reindeers in department stores at Christmas, and Whiffy McMann's name came from a friend's Christmas card. The Nyack fire department showed Elmer how the engine and hose worked, so the illustrations of the cat rescue would be correct.[181]

The educational market was still strong, and the Haders illustrated several of these books for Houghton Mifflin and Frederick A. Stokes. They still had some of their old children's pages in their files, including some that had never been published. They wrote Marion Merrill of Chicago's Merrill Publishing, suggesting some of their peep-show pages might work as a book. She replied that she had seen something similar in a New York store, and "using old material of yours is not the proper means to enter the Ten Cent publishing field." She was open to something else if they had other ideas.[182]

In spite of the many upsets in everyone's life, their city friends continued to come out to Grand View. Ernestine Evans was no longer around: she had moved to London to marry journalist Kenneth Durant. As editor of the Russian news agency TASS, he'd been deported from the U.S. ten years earlier. Marriage also had taken Bessie Beatty away: she'd married Bill Sauter, the actor she'd met on a voyage from England, and they had moved to California where he hoped to make films.

Those remaining in the city found Willow Hill an important refuge from the Depression. It was a place where one could usually relax. However, Mary Margaret remembered one time when it was anything but peaceful. Elmer had been teasing her, and she had gone up to her room. She could usually control the Irish temper she inherited from her father, but this time, as she stewed in her room, she got even madder. She threw on a raccoon coat and barged out of the room, then chased Elmer down the stairs. He hit his head on the door as he ran into the darkness to get away from this wild furry woman.

Much later she found that Elmer had to get stitches to stop the bleeding, but neither he nor Berta ever said anything to her at the time. The spat was soon forgotten. As Mary Margaret once said, "Curly-haired, brown-eyed Berta, who is the recipient of confidences never given to anybody else, is the kind of woman who remembers birthdays, little special anniversaries, and all the occasions that other people are too busy or too selfish to think about."[183] If one had a problem, big or small, it could be talked over with Berta.

Lively discussions around Elmer's hand-hewn chestnut table kept the Haders well informed about major world events, from Lindbergh's solo flight, to Gandhi's protests in India, and Hitler's rise in Germany. Jacques Marquis, their Swiss musician friend, spent most summers with the Haders, giving them glimpses into the changing world in Europe. The world peace many had worked for after the Great War began to seem impossible. Even the bucolic life in Grand View-on-Hudson took a confrontational turn.

There had been talk over the years about a bridge over the Hudson River. The nearest existing bridges were the Bear Mountain Bridge to the north, or the George Washington Bridge to the south. The only direct way to get from rural Rockland County to populous Westchester County was by ferry or by crossing over the ice bridge that usually formed in winter. Fred R. Horn, a New York State assemblyman,[184] suggested they build a toll bridge to connect the two counties. Most boosters of the bridge assumed that it would go to Piermont where there was already a factory and a railroad station.

Unfortunately, Piermont was within the twenty-five mile jurisdiction of the New York Port Authority, which was opposed to any other bridge being built besides the recently built George Washington. If one were to be built, it would have to be further north, maybe near Nyack. This was at the second-widest part of the Hudson and it seemed foolish to put it there. Besides, many residents felt the Rockland roads could not handle any more traffic, a theory reinforced by a state transportation study blaming inadequate roads for causing the deaths of two teen-agers. But in 1935 plans were drafted for a crossing between Tarrytown and Nyack, and all that seemed necessary was for the War Department to agree that the bridge would not impede river navigation. It was now an official plan, not just gossip and speculation, but Elmer, as zoning administrator, had not been notified. Nor had the neighboring town of Nyack.

Berta woke up one morning in 1936 to the sound of trees being cut down. Her trees! She immediately ran down to the source of the noise in the glen below the house. Four surveyors were cutting down the mulberry trees, and they said they were doing so on the orders of Colonel Greene of the Rockland-Westchester Hudson River Crossing Authority. She challenged them immediately about the ridiculous idea of an unneeded bridge, but they insisted it was going to be a wonderful thing for the county. "You'd be foolish to fight Colonel Greene," one man warned her. "He's a very stubborn man and he loves a battle."

"He is certainly going to have a battle," she retorted. "Pack up and get out." Like a modern Paul Revere, she set off to alert the nearby neighbors. By that time Elmer had arrived with the police chief who asked the men to show them their authority to start work on the Hader property. They refused to show him any papers, and left.[185]

By noon everyone in Grand View-on-Hudson was aroused. An attorney announced no resident needed to accept any surveyors on their property—they were trespassers. At a hastily called meeting that night the seven-man police force was doubled in size and reportedly told to shoot any surveyor on sight. These unassuming children's authors and heretofore peaceful neighbors were ready for what the *New York Times* called the "Bridge Wars."[186]

"We will keep surveyors for the bridge out of Grand View if we have to deputize every man in the village!" Elmer proclaimed. He found a New Jersey bridge expert from the Stevens Institute of Technology in nearby Hoboken, New Jersey, who asserted that it was "ridiculous to attempt to build a bridge at this point." A meeting in Upper Nyack stated the board was unalterably opposed to the construction of the so-called bridge and/or causeway. This opposition temporarily delayed the contract for the test borings.

The New York papers were told that the village of Grand View-on-Hudson was a slum and should be wiped out, but many of the people in the area who commuted to New York City were or knew influential people. The town might be old, but it was quaint and lovely. A group, including the Haders, formed a Rockland County Branch of the Hudson River Conservation Association. Four hundred residents, including actress Helen Hayes, sent a telegram to Governor Lehman protesting the bridge and urging an inquiry. They also invited him to take a ferry ride and see for himself how wide and picturesque the Tappan Zee was at this particular place.

The Haders, always verbal, argued, "The planners looked at the project only as engineers, insensitive to the local communities and what the taxpayers believed."[187]

Meanwhile, Assemblyman Fred Horn fired back, circulating petitions in favor of the bridge and accusing his opponents of being the "selfish few"—rich elitists driven by self-interest. He insisted that the residents on the east side of the Hudson were anxiously waiting to shop in Rockland County. He was able to present the governor with several petitions, containing a total of 9,000 names in favor of the bridge. The straw poll in the local newspaper favored the bridge two to one.

Mother Nature had the last word. Test borings when finally conducted showed a deep geological rift under the Tappan Zee. The borings were too deep and the cost was prohibitive.

It seemed that Colonel Greene, "the man who loved a battle" had lost his war. Grand View-on-Hudson would survive as a country haven.

CHAPTER EIGHT

WHERE DO ALL THE IDEAS COME FROM?

Berta and Elmer had spent much of the Twenties waving "Bon Voyage" from New York City's Atlantic piers, as their friends embarked on adventurous trips but never ventured on a voyage themselves. They'd stayed close to their home and work on Willow Hill. But in 1933, both Louise Seaman Bechtel and Doris Patee persuaded them to take their own trip. Winter loomed once again, and it was time to visit the friends and family who still lived on the west coast. Patee suggested they leave winter behind and go on a ship by way of the Caribbean and the Panama Canal. They'd be a different kind of tourist.

They took her advice and discovered a whole new world of tropical scenery and lively people. When they landed in Jamaica they took tours of the island and learned some of its colorful history. They heard yarns about Henry Morgan, the famous pirate who had been featured a few years before in John Steinbeck's first novel, *A Cup of Gold.* They also spent time making sketches of the area and learning about the islanders' life. When they visited the local library in Kingston, they came across a tiny old book called *The History of Tommy, A Little Black Boy of Jamaica.* It was a true story of a slave who had learned to read, was freed by his owner, and later became the island's king.

The book enthralled Elmer and Berta. It inspired them to create a story of their own about a little orphan boy, Johnny Morgan, living happily with his uncle on a farm in the Jamaican mountains. He and his friends hid from the truant officer who wished to get them in school: they felt more useful staying home, carving gourds and earning a little money from the visiting tourists. But when his aunt gave him a tiny book left by his deceased mother, Johnny decided he wanted to learn to read it and went to school to learn. Once he learned to decipher the words, he found a story about an ancestor who became a king through reading. Johnny's own reading ability opened doors to many exciting adventures and a new life, just as reading had done for his ancestor. Berta and Elmer drew charming but unsentimental pictures of a Jamaican community with real people—not the caricatures that were fairly common when tourists visited exotic countries to view "primitive" life.[188] At Patee's suggestion, they eliminated all dialect, making the book easier to read.

Since Johnny worked on a banana plantation, the Haders also visited one to get some background for what the little boy would be doing. People from the United Fruit Company were delighted to teach them about the thriving and interesting business of getting bananas to America. After *Jamaica Johnny* was on its way in 1935, they suggested to Doris Patee that they write a non-fiction book about the plantation.

As usual, editor Patee worried about the budget. The cost of full-color plates was beyond what Macmillan could pay. Maybe the Haders could contact the United Fruit Company and "persuade them to pay $1,000 toward the plates, which would be 'nothing less than a miracle.'" She pointed out that pictures of children eating bananas in the story would be worth whatever United Fruit paid for advertising—probably much more than a thousand dollars! She and the Haders were persuasive: the company eventually subsidized the costly color pictures in *Green and Gold*—a title suggested by Patee—which came out in 1936.[189]

The trip away gave them a chance to develop new ideas. Back in New York Berta and Elmer heard of a baby goat at Lockhart School in nearby Palisades. It reminded them of the many goats that lived near the top of Telegraph Hill. The school children were delighted to share their goat experiences with the Haders, and they added some of the antics they'd remembered from their San Francisco days.[190] The drawings of Telegraph Hill and the bay came from sketches and paintings from Elmer's early times in San Francisco.

Doris Patee felt *Billy Butter* would be one of their best books ever but suggested several times in the draft that they make sure that "Billy does not do actual thinking and animals *must not* talk." She also noted a few places where the incidents could be made more exciting. The finished book, which also came out in 1936, was dedicated to "Florence Babcock, a teacher at Lockhart School, where Billy Butter received his education."

Each book seemed to lead to another opportunity. After the two Jamaica books came out, they were asked to illustrate Phillis Garrard's *Banana Tree House* set in Bermuda. This also received rave reviews for its rendition of the lead character, Sukey. Unlike the many depictions common in the 1930s, the Afro-American children and families were depicted with respect and as fully developed human characters.

The release of *Jamaica Johnny* also prompted a letter from F. D. Knapp, General Manager of Albert Whitman, a publishing company in Chicago. He liked their realistic portrayal of mountain life and wanted them to illustrate a book written by Melicent Humason Lee. The dummy of *Marcos, A Mountain Boy of Mexico* was complete except for the pictures; he'd been waiting for the perfect illustrator. This story was about another little mountain boy who leaves the farm and goes off to the city to get some money to buy the team of oxen his family needs. Even though Marcos was warned that the city of Oaxaca "had too many people and not enough stars in the sky," he persisted in his quest. After serving as a weaver's apprentice for three years, he finally was able to buy a plow as well as the needed team of oxen. He returned to help his family on the farm.

Knapp hoped the Haders could illustrate it for "a fee that I can afford." Elmer suggested splitting the fee 50-50 with the author. Knapp asked if they would do it for a flat fee, and Elmer said they could—for $2,000. Knapp thought that far too high—40% of a first run of 5,000 books—and suggested instead a 5% royalty for all books sold?[191] Elmer asked for $500 down and then 5% for the first 10,000 with a 6% royalty thereafter. He also felt that the number of illustrations Whitman wanted would justify a first run of 20,000 copies. The Haders had previously committed to two spring books and a fall one but thought they could promise delivery of *Marcos* the following June or July. Knapp and publisher Whitman eventually agreed to the Haders' terms, and the book came out in 1937 to good reviews.

A trip to visit Elmer's brother, Waldo, led to more inspirations for western stories. Waldo and his wife Fanita ran a grocery store in the small town of Lander, Wyoming, just south of the Wind River Mountain range. He loved the countryside around him and really wanted his brother to come out and visit where "men are men and smell like horses." He was active in the town's civic activities and kept thinking of ideas for local stories, which Berta and Elmer could write and illustrate.

There were two tribes of Indians on the reservation near Lander: the Shoshone, native to the area, and the Northern Arapahoe. An 1868 Indian treaty left these Arapahoe without a land base, so the federal government moved them to the reservation with the Shoshones.[192] Waldo suggested the Haders write a story about the problem of an educated Indian mother trying to raise her children on a reservation where the elders obstructed and ridiculed her efforts to teach her children to be "anything other than Indian." He also informed the Haders that the current Arapahoe chief lamented the fact that the oldest Indians were rapidly dying off and no record was being made of the history of the Sun Dance. After Waldo found there already was a book about it in the Columbian Museum, he promised he could provide plenty of other stories if they would visit Lander: maybe one about the fawn and the Irish Wolfhound who'd been bottle fed together on a nearby ranch. Now full-grown, they wandered the mountains together, and Waldo thought he could arrange for the Haders to see the two.

After Berta and Elmer purchased a new Buick in 1934—complete with a radio and a heater—they drove out to Wyoming. They had a wonderful time and enjoyed meeting Waldo's wife, Fanita, and their daughter Jean. The area was very different from what they were used to, and they happily sketched Indians, cowboys, and horses. The Appaloosas fascinated them both: there had been a little spotted horse on the Monterey ranch Elmer visited as a child. They also sketched pictures of the area, and left after a wonderful and inspiring visit.

The return to Grand View brought a new awareness of all that was going on in Europe. The weekenders recounted many stories of the terrors developing in Germany, as Hitler became the German chancellor known as "Der Fuhrer." Most of the journalists did not share the admiration of such influential Americans as Henry Ford and Charles Lindbergh. However, the German invasion of Czechoslovakia in 1937 horrified those who had hoped Hitler would confine his regime to Germany. It was obvious he had far larger plans. Meanwhile, in Russia, Stalin's purges eliminated those who disagreed with him—upsetting many who had once envisioned the development of an egalitarian country after the overthrow of the Czar in 1917.

Regardless of what they learned about world events from the visits of friends, or from the newspapers and radio, Berta and Elmer chose to ignore the upside down world of the 1930s. No worrisome events found their way into the books they were writing and illustrating. The Hader books at this time concentrate on America as a good place, where children as well as adults expected to pitch in to help the family. The Farmer in the Dell, with a young father as the farmer, has no mention of the Dust Bowl or the Midwest drought, both cataclysms affecting huge swaths of the American Heartland. Berta and Elmer felt children needed a sense of stability, and consequently illustrated a world where animals and people worked together.

Meanwhile, they continued to work with other editors. Having seen how many copies of educational books were sold, they created a book of safety tips in *Stop, Look, and Listen*. *Kirkus Reviews* felt it would be useful in every classroom, even though, "It seems somewhat machine made; and is not up to the Haders' usual standard of spontaneity, either in text or pictures."

Elmer continued to create occasional dust jackets. The ones he most enjoyed were for John Steinbeck's California books. John Steinbeck had seen a copy of *Billy Butter* in a bookshop, and was taken by the illustrations, which pictured California so well. He told his editor at Viking—Milton B. Glick—to get Hader to do the dust jacket for his next book. Hader said he liked Steinbeck's work, and was sure he could create one to suit. The painting for *The Long Valley* went easily.

However, for *The Grapes of Wrath* it was harder to match the artist's vision with that of the editor. Elmer submitted six sketches, two of which Glick liked. After much back and forth about what elements the editor liked and what he didn't, Elmer finally submitted two paintings. Steinbeck and Glick both loved the painting with the Joads and a trail of other dust bowl refugees looking over the California valley. Viking created a wrap-around jacket for the book that "became the most widely-recognized iconic image of the Dust Bowl migration of the 1930s."[193] Elmer was paid a total of $75 for the painting—no residuals. He went on to paint the jackets for two more of Steinbeck's California books: *East of Eden* (1952) and *Winter of Our Discontent* (1961).

CHAPTER NINE

"BERTANELMER"—WORKING TOGETHER

Their next book was based on their trips to Maine, where Bessie Beatty and husband, Bill Sauter, had purchased a large property, Green Gables. *Tommy Thatcher Goes to Sea* was dedicated to Betty (Bessie's nickname) "in memory of many wonderful trips on the Maine coast." Doris Patee, who felt the book was WAY too long at 33,000 words, heavily edited this book. If there were seven chapters, she wrote, none should be over ten pages. Might Elmer cut some of the captain's stories? The Haders agreed to most of her suggestions, though they quibbled with some suggestions about the language being too odd and salty. In one spot where her critique noted that "Tommy says 'Gosh!' pretty often." Elmer told her that Tommy really used stronger language but some folks are squeamish.

Under Patee's guidance, the Haders did such a good job with *Tommy Thatcher* that Hilda McLeod, the secretary of the Maine

State Library, sent them a letter offering to include them in the Maine Author Collection.[194] The Haders wrote back "hoping that the little incident of being born elsewhere" would not bar them from the honor and sending the library a gift autographed copy of the book including one of their special watercolor dedicatory pages. They also mentioned that many of the backgrounds in the book had been painted in the little village of West Point. The library's secretary wrote back she was "breathless with appreciation of the special page, appreciated their feeling of "warmth for the state, and hope they would continue visiting." They apparently never made the roster of Maine authors. However, their picture-book map of Maine became part of the 2014 official Maine atlas.[195]

By this time the Haders were often referred to as one: "Bertanelmer." They began to sign their letters to friends this way and felt their lives had become totally united. They had worked together ever since Elmer had been mustered out of the army, and their ideas for the future had been cemented together by their search for a place to live. Long walks gave them plenty of time to talk over their visions for the future, and come to agreement about both the big and the little plans. Then when Elmer joined Berta in creating magazine pages, the two found it easy to work together.

As Berta later told Mary Margaret McBride, neither of them were the type that enjoyed arguments. When McBride pressed for a story about a disagreement, they could recall only one serious enough that they slept in separate rooms for three days. It had been over something embarrassingly silly. Elmer would often read a current book to Berta as she prepared dinner. This night the book happened to be a current best seller, *Kristin Lavransdatter,* set in medieval Sweden. Berta was so into the story she was upset when Kristin's husband lashed out with his whip hitting Kristin. Elmer tried to calm her down, telling her to "give the man a chance." This inflamed Berta once more—no man should be given a second chance to hit his wife —so she flounced off into the other bedroom and refused to talk to him for three days. After that long a span neither of them could recall why they had acted that way, and they quietly reconciled.

There were minor disagreements of course, such as when to return from a winter trip: Berta wanted to get back early to get to work in the garden, while Elmer preferred to "stay in the land of sunshine until the middle of April."[196] These squabbles were usually solved quickly. Berta later said she felt that the important foundation for a successful marriage was in liking the same things—animals, friends, home, work, et cetera. That made it easy to accommodate each other.[197] In one letter to Doris, Elmer begins the letter by grousing about the gray and overcast skies. Then he apologizes for the grumble . . . "you would think I had gotten up on the wrong side of the bed. Tain't so. I feel chipper as a lark and I couldn't get out of the wrong side of the bed anyway. Berta blocks all traffic that way."

The fact that the Haders were so compatible probably was one reason why so many of their friends found it pleasant on Willow Hill. Rose Wilder Lane seems to have been one of the few who couldn't find peace around the big chestnut table. She'd long blamed Berta for hiding—and losing—her contract with Frederick O'Brien. She was irritated when her old Telegraph Hill friends talked of O'Brien as being a best-selling author, even though they knew about the editing she had done and the way he'd treated her.[198] And after visiting many Midwest wheat farms for a *Saturday*

Evening Post article, she became more and more suspicious of programs promising the "greatest good for the greatest number."

Rose had met too many marginal farmers who lost their farms. She blamed the losses on Franklin Roosevelt's regulations and government programs. Even genial Lem Parton couldn't calm her down. Since journalist Ernestine Evans had worked for the New Deal when it was just getting started, and Mary Margaret McBride was a great fan of the Roosevelts, the disagreements became uncomfortable. Rose dropped out of the Hader circle. Although she bought a house and lived in nearby Danbury, Connecticut, she apparently never visited Willow Hill again.[199] Berta found it hard to lose her long-time friend and roommate, but finally accepted that their interests had diverged.

As more of their jointly illustrated and authored books appeared in stores, the question always arose, "Who does what? Who is the artist, and who is the author?"

Elmer insisted they worked as one, sharing completely in their books' creation. One would get the first idea, and they'd talk about it, each adding to the original. They said they worked out the "thought sketches" together. Once the story idea was formed, Elmer often worked on the drafts outdoors pounding "away on his venerable machine, doing his best work when the sky was blue, sunshine trickling down between leaves, birds singing . . .." From then on they would work together creating the dummies, book-form layouts of text and rough sketches. The finished illustrations were by both: Elmer would sketch out the completed drawing they'd worked out, and then Berta would add details and give them a tighter, smoother look. Certainly the finished pictures reflected their long training and practice in two very different fields of art. As they worked, they learned and benefited from each other.

Finally, in 1937, they planned and produced a delightful little book, *Working Together: The Inside Story of The Hader Books,* explaining how they actually did work together. The cover was done in Berta's careful script, with the round upright letters common on many of their Macmillan books. Macmillan handed these little hardcovers out free for publicity at most library and publishing conventions. May Massee wrote that she'd "giggled her way from page to page—it is the cleverest publicity I've ever seen."

The charming sketches show them creating the manuscript for *Tommy Thatcher*. Together they puzzle over ideas and write the chapters together. Then they finally carry a huge manuscript into the editor's office. Pictures show the editor and assistants taking turns in cutting out parts of the manuscript until it returns in a just a tiny envelope. This delightful handout never really answered the question for those who didn't believe two persons could act as one, but it certainly showcased their humor and their attention to the interesting details that could catch a reader's eye.

It still seemed impossible that they could work so collaboratively. Many other artist couples were working together: Miska and Maude Petersham, Ingri and Edgar d'Aulaire, and Clement and Edith Hurd. But none seemed to share their words and art with each other as Berta and Elmer did. Niece Joy Hoerner Rich remembers visiting them and watching them pass papers back and forth as they worked at adjoining easels. "What do you think?" Elmer might ask as he gave his latest drawing to his wife. "Well, perhaps it needs a little more detail here," Berta would answer, and then Elmer would say, "Well, then just 'Berta' it up."[200]

The Depression had forced libraries, like publishers, to cut budgets, but librarians were still a major influence in children's book publishing. Parents and teachers still wanted to buy the best for their children, and librarians' recommendations and newspaper reviews helped them choose. The Newbery Awards brought many outstanding books for older children into prominence, and some felt the artists of children's picture books should also be singled out for their work.

Children's librarians had long recognized the importance of good art in picture books. The illustrations not only reinforced and gave meaning to the text, but they often stayed in the person's memory throughout life. For many children these might be their only exposure to the arts.

Publisher Frederic Melcher, the man behind the Newbery Award, chose to name the new medal after the nineteenth century artist Randolph Caldecott. Caldecott's lively pictures had been popular in the early 1800s, and his illustrations of William Cowper's poem *John Gilpin's Ride* were popular with young and old. The chaos caused by the once-dignified merchant on his runaway horse careening through the English countryside gives the viewer much to look at and enjoy as every person and animal goes scrambling out of the way. The sense of motion is evident even in the small reproduction of the ride on the front of the medal.

Since buyers were eager to buy books with a shiny gold Newbery medal sticker on the cover, knowing they were outstanding, publishers were enthusiastic about this new picture book award. They assumed—rightly—that it would call attention to picture books and increase sales.

After much discussion, it was decided the criteria for the Caldecott would be based on only the illustrations of the text, no matter what the latter might be. The gold first place medal would be presented to the illustrator, not the author. There would be only one prizewinner, but the finalists would be named as runners-up. (A few years later it was decided to rename these books retroactively as Honor Books, and these received a silver medal with the same design.) As with the Newbery, publishers would send their best candidates to the American Library Association for reviews by their committee.

The criteria for the Caldecott Medal meant the art in picture books was now considered to be an important component of children's literature. It gave a boost to both publishers and authors after the troubles of the Depression era.

The first Caldecott Award was given in 1938. All three winners were well-known artists of the time. Two of the three books, published by Lippincott, did not have original texts, but in terms of the award, this was not necessary. Helen Dean Fish, the children's book editor at Frederick Stokes, had been thinking about a book on *Animals of the Bible* for many years. She provided the text, asking Dorothy Lathrop to choose the animals and do the illustrations. The elegant animals and enticing black and white illustrations enhanced the biblical texts on the facing pages. Helen Dean Fish had also selected the nursery rhymes for the runner-up, *Four and Twenty Blackbirds*, and chosen Robert Lawson as the illustrator. Boris Artzybashof was the second runner-up: he retold and illustrated one of his native folk tales: *Seven Simeons: A Russian Tale*. Previously, he had illustrated the 1928 Newbery Award winner, *Gay-Neck, the Story of a Pigeon*.

The next year six books made it onto the committee's final list. *Mei Li* by Thomas Handforth was an imagined story of a real little girl the artist met while living in China. Louise Seaman had chosen him many years before to be the illustrator for one of Elizabeth Coatsworth's picture books, and Ned Bechtel, Louise Seaman's husband, had collected his etchings for some years. This book was a surprise because the artist chose woodblocks to illustrate *Mei Li*, believing the style was more appropriate to the setting. The five other artists chosen as the runners-up were also familiar names: James Daugherty, Clare Turlay Newberry, Laura Adams Armer, Wanda Gág, and Robert Lawson.

In the same year, 1939, the Haders published another animal story to editor Patee's delight. Ever since she had taken over for Louise Seaman, she had encouraged the Haders to focus on one big book a year, rather than many small ones and felt they should concentrate more on animal stories. She accepted their many other ideas, but felt their strength was in their art, and it should be focused on the animals which they drew so well.

The tale of *Cock-A-Doodle Doo, The Story of a Little Red Rooster* is simple—an egg hatches a little chick instead of a duckling, much to the other ducklings' astonishment. Mother Duck does her best to turn this baby into a proper chicken to no avail. He decides to find his way to a neighboring farm where he hears other chickens. The reader watches the chick's progress through the changing backgrounds on every page. The illustrations give life and emotion to the story, from the surprised faces of the ducklings to the fearful two-page spread with a huge black hawk swooping down from the sky, talons extended. Elmer believed that if "an artist must choose between emotion and technique, he would be well to choose the former." They always tried to make their stories ring true.[201]

The Hader art as well as Patee's skill in editing combined to produce excellent results. They watched as the early Caldecott Medals went to other artists, many of whom were friendly rivals. However, in 1940, *Cock-A-Doodle Doo* was named one of the runners-up.[202]

Doris wrote that it was "a *very* close runner-up for the Caldecott Medal this year and personally I was heart-broken that it didn't make the grade. I know these awards don't mean as much to you as to some people, but you deserve one of them and I want you to have it." Elmer replied that Berta was "relieved considerably that the book did not rate a medal. As for me, I don't think little Red's tail feathers will droop . . .."[203]

"We do our best each year but when the last word is said, and the last touch put on the final illustration, there is little anyone can do but pray . . . we will take what comfort we can out of the old saying by Confucius, 'Always a runner-up but never a medalist keep big slob sheriff from door.' Vive le runner-up."[204]

✧ CHAPTER TEN ✦

WARTIME!

The Haders received the Caldecott runner-up award for *Cock-a-Doodle-Doo* in 1940. It was the last year of peace for the United States. Elmer wrote in answer to a letter requesting some facts about their publishing history that "we are horrified at the reports that fill the air and papers of the insane happening in the world today. We are firm believers that war never has and never will be anything but a destructive force that settles nothing. Fortunately, we are able to get away from the mad world about us and seek calm in the creative world of children's books."[205] They tried to pass on this peaceful feeling to young readers.

Asia Magazine changed owners: Richard Walsh and his wife Pearl Buck turned it from being a travel magazine promoting trade with China to a magazine concentrating on international affairs. There was major interest in the second Sino-Japanese war that was still going on. Elsie Weil left her job as the managing editor and became a free-lance writer. Mary Margaret McBride turned her CBS radio show over to Bessie Beatty and moved to NBC radio.

Besides war stories from faraway China between the Nationalists and the Communists, stories about the various atrocities in Europe were reaching the United States. When Germany began bombing British cities, President Franklin D. Roosevelt wanted to support Prime Minister Winston Churchill but recognized that the country was not yet ready to go to war. However, he did allow the United Kingdom to get supplies from the United States under a "Lend-Lease" program. The warfare in the Atlantic was already impacting America, since German submarines were attacking U. S. merchant ships, and the Navy was attacking German submarines. Women were knitting "Bundles for Britain," and young men were going to Canada to enlist in the British forces.

The illustrations in Mary Margaret McBride's autobiographical book, *How Dear to My Heart,* looked back to a more peaceful time in the Midwest. And even though *The Cat and the Kitten* is not about the Haders, the pictures show the comfortable living room at Willow Hill, with Elmer quietly reading, Berta knitting peacefully, and a kitten tangling in the yarn.

The Haders' next book, *Little Town,* in 1941 continued this theme of a simpler time. The Haders planned a layout similar to 1930's *The Farmer in the Dell*, believing the two books were comparable in portraying predictable lives. Life in the town proceeds according to the hours in the day, as life on the farm correlates with the seasons of the year.

The hands on the town clock in the village square announce the hour as people wake, go to school or work, or take the train for a commute to the city. Loosely based on surrounding towns, it shows the residents moving through their day. Homes, workplaces, markets, town meetings, and community events are clearly portrayed. The book provided a perfect antidote to the disturbing news from Europe, portraying a delightful, small American town in which everyone works together. A parade and the volunteer firemen putting out a fire provide the only excitement. The details in each workplace—bank, market, hardware store—are so precise that one reviewer suggested it was a perfect book for teaching foreigners to read commonplace English words. Most pictured items are named in the text, and all are totally recognizable. That feature was good for young American readers, too.

Their editor, Doris Patee, told the Haders that the original book, *The Farmer in the Dell*, was an "impractical and expensive layout," and she wished they had conferred with her about the proposed layout before dropping off their dummy for *Little Town*. Nevertheless, she did her best to fit the Haders' plan into the current publishing realities. The book could have only 88 pages, not 96, and her letter listed the changes to make it work out. She combined some activities on one page and suggested moving others to different parts of the day, to ensure the color pages would fall in the right spots. The book jacket and end papers would be in four colors, as they were in the farm book. After all these suggestions, she wound up saying it was a grand idea for a book and she expected it would set sales records.[206]

Elmer and Berta responded that "in planning the book we made a list of the various businesses and activities that are to be found in practically all small towns in the forty-eight states. Then we began the task of fitting the list into the ninety-six page dummy to match the other. It might be that we could work out a completely different layout and eliminate the double spreads . . ..." They went on to list twenty-six items they had omitted in the dummy, and hoped the problems would be smoothed out. Between letters and visits, their differing ideas meshed into the final book.

In October, Patee wrote the Haders that the printed and bound copies were almost ready for delivery. However, "for some unknown reason which drives me crazy, the printers seem to have separated that lovely double-spread of the parade . . . the Glasers are always so careful that it is hard to believe something like this could slip through." She continued that, "*Little Town* is a swell book and I hope you will otherwise feel very happy about it."[207] Elmer responded "that often happens to parades . . . but it wouldn't be a bad idea to make the pages uniform in the next edition."[208] In regard to Patee's talk about the next book, he wrote, "soon the seat of the pants will contact the seat of the creative chair in the studio and a bigger . . . no, I mean better book will emerge for 1942."

Shortly after *Little Town* came out during the fall publishing period, the Japanese bombed Pearl Harbor. The next day, 8 December 1941, Franklin Roosevelt asked Congress to declare war on Japan, and Congress passed a declaration of war against Japan immediately. Three days later, both Italy and Germany declared war on the United States. The United States reciprocated, and the country was immediately on a war footing. Both Republicans and Democrats announced they would work together to defeat the enemy. Political maneuvering was to be put on hold until the war was over.

The war effort wrought many changes in farms, small towns, and cities across the country. The Roosevelt Administration created many government boards and gave them powers to match their mandates. Top businessmen were recruited to run these major boards, agreeing to accept only a dollar a year for their services. Rationing began almost immediately, with rubber first on the list, since that was a commodity the U.S. could not produce at home.

Tires, cars, and bicycles became unobtainable for ordinary citizens, and even galoshes, shoes with rubber soles, and elastic in waistbands disappeared. People saved rubber bands. One woman remembered her dad carefully slicing up the fingers in the rubber gloves he used in his work in order to make rubber bands. Since leather to repair shoe soles was unavailable, insoles were cut out from cardboard and fitted into holey shoes. Vehicles were required to have stickers posted on their windshields showing their particular gas allowance in a given time period.

Most foods were also rationed including beef, sugar, coffee, and butter. Everyone, whether adult or child, received a ration book with their individual allotment of food and clothing. Every town had its own ration board, run by volunteer citizens. Elmer agreed to be on the Ration Board for Grand View. Still, Jane Barrow wrote that "Berta Hader refused to apply for a ration card . . . she felt the processing of persons by numbers was the beginning of regimentation for all of us."[209]

Elmer also volunteered as Air Raid Warden. These wardens, like many other citizens, memorized the silhouettes of German planes. It wasn't an empty threat: there were reports of German submarines (called U-boats) landing soldiers on nearby Long Island, and many European towns had been decimated by bomb-caused fires. The wardens also enforced blackouts, making sure that no light from any house or business leaked into the night. Light could pinpoint a target for German pilots, or provide a background of light on the land that would serve to silhouette the darker profiles of ships at sea. The blackouts inspired a popular 1942 song by singer Vaughn Monroe, "When the Lights Go on Again All Over the World."

The war made radio listening a major part of everyone's life, even though war news in newspapers and radio broadcasts was censored. Still, radio programs by Mary Margaret McBride and Bessie Beatty gave glimpses into the lives of the people who were now involved in the war, one way or another. Mary Margaret's program provided a link between the small towns sacrificing on the fringes and the people involved in the center of things.

Berta and Elmer continued with their writing and illustration. They illustrated two Burke Boyce historical books for Viking: *The Perilous Night* and *Stronghold*. A War Production Board (WPB) was put in charge of the country's resources, allocating them to the companies that could produce the items required for fighting the war. Some companies were unable to get the materials they wanted for the things they used to make but were assigned other items that were needed.

The Haders had always tried to be self-sufficient for the most part, and this was now the goal for everyone. Besides all the volunteer service work already being done by busy wives and mothers, "Victory Gardens" were added to the list of chores. Households were encouraged to grow and preserve fruits and vegetables for the future—all commercial canned goods were rationed for civilians in order to provide them to the soldiers. Community parks and other unused spaces were turned into garden plots for those who didn't have land available. Gardeners like Berta, who had always had a vegetable garden, shared their expertise with others.

A "luxury tax" was imposed on any purchase deemed unnecessary. Even school children felt that tax, because movie tickets were considered a luxury. There was always newsreel of what was going on overseas and also clips of glamorous film stars dancing with enlisted men at the United Servicemen's Organization (USO) or selling Savings War Bonds. Bonds had been used to raise money for the war effort in the First World War, where it was found to be a way to enforce savings, control the money supply, and encourage patriotism. The new bonds cost $18.75 each, and could be redeemed ten years later for $25.00—an easy example of interest. Those who couldn't scrape up the $18.75 to purchase a bond could buy war stamps for as little as ten cents each to be pasted into a stamp book. When the books showed enough stamps had been purchased to buy a war bond, the book was turned in for the bond itself. School children bought their stamps in school, where large posters showed how many bonds were needed to buy a jeep or a tank. A group of Sea Scouts deposited the money they were saving toward a sailboat into a War Bond—they planned to buy their boat after the war was over.

There were constant drives to collect items needed for the war. This was one in which children helped. All kinds of scrap metals were collected, including the small amounts of tinfoil in cigarette and gum packages. Children carefully rolled the foil into balls and also collected newspapers, magazines, and other miscellaneous paper for paper drives that even included correspondence—all letters sent to Mary Margaret McBride at radio station WOR, for example, went to a paper mill, not to archives.[210]

The publishing business was also affected. Patee wrote the Haders in 1942 that the war situation was holding up the contracts:

they had to put a "war escape clause" in the contracts and until that was settled they couldn't send a contract for the new book. That little item didn't stop the Haders from working on their next project based on brother Waldo's idea for a book about American Indians.

Publishers and authors were asked to turn in metal plates for books that had not been reprinted in the past two years. The Hader's *Picture Book of the States* fell into this category, and its plates, too, went to the government metal stockpile to be melted down for ammunition. Paper allowances were cut resulting in trimmed page sizes, thinner paper, and smaller books like the "Big Little Books" for children and "Pocket Books" for adults. These had arrived on the market before the war, but now became widely distributed. The acidic paper used was of poor quality, turning brown and crumbling in a very few years. Doris Patee wrote the Haders, "Personally I don't feel as disturbed about book materials as some other people do, for it seems to me that there is even a challenge and a fascination in trying to do the best we can with what we have available."[211]

Most people rose to the challenge to make do. With the country's young men being drafted, women discovered they could do "men's work" as they filled the vacant jobs. Scrap drives, rationing, and credit limitations affected nearly everyone. Young and old had a personal stake in the war effort. As Jane Barrow recounted, the war also brought division into the Haders' group of friends. Gertrude Emerson's uncle "was a fascist who worked at it," while long-time friends Stella Karn and Elsie Weil were Jewish. Berta and Elmer found it a difficult period as they tried to keep the peace among the different factions.[212] They must have done a fairly good job because Elsie Weil later wrote them a thank you note for the good conversation and companionship of the weekend.

Berta and Elmer continued their weekend hospitality during the war years. People they knew from many places often came through New York on assignments. Willow Hill was close to the little Erie train from New York City, so friends and relatives from other faraway places could stop by for short or long visits. Berta must have sympathized when her niece, Joy Hoerner Rich, came to the East Coast to be with her new husband until he left for overseas. She couldn't return to Oregon until she saved enough gasoline ration stamps to drive the three thousand miles back to Oregon, so was able to spend six weeks with them during this period. It gave her a chance to enjoy some of the weekend friends and also to watch the Haders at work.

At that time they were finally developing the book suggested long before by Louise Seaman—*The Little Stone House* was a simplified version of how they had built their own home. Joy watched them pass the sketches and final pictures back and forth to each other as they painted. Each completed picture was a totally joint creation, as the two had been insisting for years.

Many of their friends in the city often worked long hours in stressful jobs and needed these time-outs in the country. Hamilton Williamson, though aging and slower, came with her usual supply of amusing stories. Kenneth Durant had severed his relationship with the USSR's newspaper, TASS, remarried a poet, and retired to a farm in Vermont. And it seemed as if every visitor brought someone else. Jane Barrow said she never could understand how Berta could manage feeding people so effortlessly, especially with the rationing, while she herself felt stressed when planning meals for only herself and her husband.[213] Friends who came for weekends with the Haders often brought some of their own rations to share; one weekend two legs of lamb showed up. Berta hurriedly dispatched Joy to hide one of the legs in the garage in order to avoid embarrassment. It was cold enough to freeze the lamb so it could be used for another occasion.

Other friends were very far away. One good friend, former editor Gertrude Emerson, had married an Indian scholar, Boshi Sen, and was now living there, writing about the country and Mahatma Gandhi's peaceful protests against British rule.

Notes continued to come from these friends, describing the Christmases spent at Nyack in the big room with the fire and the candles and the African violets on the windowsill, and good things to eat coming from the kitchen. The memory was cherished.

Shortly after Joy left, the weekenders had something to celebrate. Elsie Weil, long a fixture at Willow Hill celebrations, finished the book she was co-authoring with one of her friends, Margaret Landon. Margaret based her book on the diary of an English woman who went to far away Siam as a governess, and Elsie had learned much about the country from working at *Asia* Magazine. *Anna and the King of Siam* was published in 1944, and Americans were happy to read a book about Asian culture in more glamorous times.[214]

Among the Hader visitors were two young women from India, nieces of Jawaharlal Nehru. He was part of Mahatma Gandhi's independence movement, as was his sister, Vijaya Lakshmi Pandit and her husband. Both were often imprisoned when their children were young. When the Pandit's teenage daughter, Lekha, was imprisoned, it meant she and her younger sister, Neyantara, could never go to college in India. The Pandits made arrangements for their daughters to travel alone on a troopship to Wellesley College in Massachusetts. No information was ever given out ahead of time on where or when the troopships were going, and this one landed in California, instead of on the East coast. Their mother, Madame Pandit, had given them sound advice: "The thing to remember," she said, "is to look helpless, but be efficient. That way everybody gives you a helping hand, and if everybody doesn't, you can take care of yourself anyway."[215] Helping hands got them on to New York, where they also became Hader visitors.

Tara, in her memoir *Prisons and Chocolate Cake,* wrote that

> One weekend we went to Nyack, near New York, where we stayed with a charming couple who wrote and illustrated children's books. It was a peaceful two days in the cool green countryside, where we had a chance to rest from the heat and noise of the city. We realized that there were places in America where people lived at a leisurely pace. Our hostess' young nephew, Richard, was home on leave from the navy, and we had long talks and exchanged ideas with him. We found that young Americans knew very little about India, particularly what was happening in India at that time.

> 'That's not hard to understand,' said Richard. 'Why, right here in the States, a New Yorker knows very little about Texas, and vice versa. How can we know about a foreign country when we don't know our own?' When we told Richard about the political situation at home and how thousands of people were in jail for wanting their country's freedom, he looked at us in consternation. It was a revelation to him.

> He was indignant. 'That could never happen here. A person can go right up to the White House and say 'Mr. Roosevelt, I think you're

an old stinker and nobody could do anything to him except maybe throw him out of the White House.' He ended with a chuckle, and we laughed with Richard at the idea of such unrestrained freedom of speech.[216]

Although the Pandits felt Americans knew little about their country, Berta and Elmer were ones who did. Their wide-ranging interests and well-traveled friends told them much about the world outside Willow Hill. Like most Americans, they listened to the radio and read the newspapers. In 1944 there was news about the successful landing of the Allied forces on the French beaches and their long slog inland fighting the Germans every step of the way.

They felt personally involved when Art Rich, the husband of niece Joy who had visited them so recently, was taken prisoner during the Battle of the Bulge. As the Allied soldiers took over the German-occupied land, more and more stories of Nazi brutality leaked out, and anyone who knew a soldier or prisoner of war—which was nearly everybody—found more and more to worry about. Berta saved a typewritten quote from author Lloyd Alexander, who summed up their feelings about war. "Each day of war takes us further from all we could hope to be or do. We gain nothing but heartbreak, and lose everything we cherish. Our lives erode and diminish, our children see no future except a calendar of anguish and death. Our only hope for tomorrow is for peace now."[217]

The Haders felt that children needed to see a happier future. Those subjected to violence—whether real or only heard about— needed to find a refuge in books, just as their friends needed the peaceful haven of Willow Hill. Children also needed to learn the rules of civilized behavior, which meant thinking of others instead of only themselves. Most of the Hader books portrayed children realizing they were part of their family and community, recognizing their own strengths and capabilities, and shaping their own futures.

Their next book was based on a trip they had taken to the small mountain village of Taxco in Mexico. The lively pictures add life and color to the exciting story of a small Mexican boy in *The Story of Pancho and the Bull with the Crooked Tail* (1942). The owner of the largest ranch in the village wants to capture a raging bull that is ruining his herds. He promises prizes including a bag of gold to anyone who can capture him. Many fine strapping men compete to win the prizes, but the bull always gets away. Then little Pancho uses his creativity—and good luck—to tie the bull to a large tree and win the money for his family.

Waldo's comment about the Indian view of education as learning by doing, rather than books, inspired them to rewrite a 1932 manuscript that had been rejected by Scribner's about a little Indian boy and the animals he meets that persuade him they are too small to be worth his attention. Their new pictures were full of emotion. The reader immediately identifies with Little Brave Heart, pictured on the opening page of *The Mighty Hunter*. Every picture is full of motion. Every expression on each animal he intends to shoot tells its own story, and the reader can't wait for the final conclusion, where the bear chases Little Brave Heart into the school house. A perfect conclusion.

Again, there were changes in the printing process . . . this time in the colors. Patee wrote that fluorescent colors saved money: "If we did the book like Pancho, the book would have had to have less color or flat color, or work on celluloid, etc. etc. This method gives us the approximation of a process job for much less money."[218]

In a later biographical note about herself to an interested teacher, Berta mentioned she'd become interested in Indian art during her childhood through reading books by Ernest Thompson Seton and through studying the designs of Indian beadwork at the public library. She would then design bags and chains and watch fobs in beadwork or feathers or on a loom. "I spent hours making gifts for the family and my friends and even executed a few orders from the same friend of my mother's who had purchased the Sunbonnet babies."[219] Because of Elsie Weil's love of the west, they dedicated the book to "Sakotari: Glacier Woman from Tree Woman and River Boy." Weil was absolutely thrilled. She had loved Indian names after a trip west to Glacier Park and long ago nicknamed Berta "Tree Woman," while Elmer became "River Boy."[220]

In 1944, *The Mighty Hunter* received a runner-up award from the Caldecott Committee because of the wonderful and authentic illustrations. Doris Patee had hoped for the gold medal but was pleased her major authors now had their second Caldecott Award. Berta preferred to stay out of the limelight. She confided to Jane Barrow that every time they made an appearance, she had to find something to wear from the inside out. Her comfortable home garb of peasant dress and kerchief just wouldn't do.[221]

That same year they also acted on Louise Seaman's suggestion from long ago that they write about the building of their house. An imaginary family decides to build its own house, from the ground up. Each member—mom, dad, and the two children—works hard clearing the lot, building the foundation, and carrying the boards, while countless little animals hide in the landscape watching the activities. Berta pointed out the book certainly did not show the many backaches that developed during the building, and it didn't dwell on all the problems the Haders had faced.

It did portray their strong conviction that you can always get what you want through hard work. The happy ending has the family settled snugly in *The Little Stone House*, and a large two-page spread shows the family celebrating Thanksgiving with a large circle of friends. Although Berta and Elmer said the book was not based on real people, most of those in the large Thanksgiving group around the big chestnut table are the Hader crowd.

Though they didn't know it then, 1944 turned out to be an opportune time for publishing this book. The European war was close to being over, and two years later when it was over, every ex-soldier and family would be looking for a house.

The radio brought the news to Willow Hill that President Franklin Roosevelt died unexpectedly in April 1945. That was grim news for many, whether they liked him or not. The country was still at war, after all. Vice President Harry S. Truman immediately became president. Very little was known about him, except he had been a haberdasher in Missouri, and he seemed a very small man for the large job of winning the war.

Before Roosevelt died, he had attended a conference with Joseph Stalin and Winston Churchill about plans for peace after the war was over. Germany surrendered on 7 May, less than a month after Roosevelt's death. Four months later President Truman authorized the dropping of atomic bombs on Hiroshima and Nagasaki, and Japan also surrendered.

The day "when the lights come on again all over the world" finally arrived in 1945. The war was over. There were impromptu gatherings all over the United States. The troops and all the prisoners of war would now be coming home. Peace was here, once again.

→ CHAPTER ELEVEN ←

THE CALDECOTT MEDAL AND AFTER

$\mathcal{A}$fter the continuing success of *Little Town*, Doris felt there should be a similar book about life in the big city. The Haders agreed to do it, after they finished the projects already scheduled. First they really wanted to do *Rainbow's End*, another Maine story. It was about a sea captain who had drawn several plans for his dream retirement home and who finally found the perfect spot to build it. He sets up his temporary tent and goes into town for supplies. Each time he goes into town, his time is taken up with somebody else's project, so he still has no house when winter arrives. He decides to go back to sea, but while he's away looking for a job, the townspeople use his own plans to build his house at Rainbow's End. The dedication, to Latrobe (Toby) and Ruth Carroll, suggests that the captain might be based on Toby, who had certainly given up many weekends to help the Haders build the "Little Stone House."

Just before the Second World War Berta and Elmer had visited the "Futurama" exhibits at the 1939 New York World's Fair. The Fair's theme was "The World of Tomorrow." The Haders rode on the conveyor belt through the exhibit, looking down through a curved glass pane at a model city with topographic features and futuristic highways. It seemed a good time to write about the future, so they created *Skyrocket,* a story about a boy who gets a chance to help a pilot deliver mail around the world in one twenty-four-hour day. *Skyrocket* shows some of the world's countries from a view high above the earth, but the pictures include many little features that children delight to discover. The Haders enjoyed learning about other places and thought American children would as well. Some of the World's Fair ideas were being put into practice in New York City, and perhaps they could show these off.

When Louise Seaman Bechtel, their former editor, wrote a delightful little book based loosely on her husband Ned's collection of animals, *Mr. Peck's Pets*, she asked Berta and Elmer to do the illustrations. Of course, neither Doris Patee nor the Haders could pass up that project from their close friends. They put off working on *The Big City* until they had finished the book for Louise and Ned. Since they knew the Mt. Kisco farm and the various animals, it was a fun book to do.

The sudden death of Bessie Beatty in April, 1947 was another highly emotional interruption. She had been a part of their lives since Telegraph Hill days when Bessie encouraged Berta's work at the *Bulletin*. She'd found a job for Berta when she went to New York City to wait for Elmer's return from World War One and had helped them buy their property on Willow Hill. Her absence left a real void at the big chestnut table, but her husband, Bill Sauter, continued to come as an accepted member of the Hader circle.

Work always helped. They had *The Big City* to complete. The storyline for this book has an uncle visiting New York City and learning about it from his nephew and niece. The family takes him to many of New York's star attractions, while showing him how they and their parents live, work, and play. Along with *The Farmer in the Dell* and *Little Town,* the three give a nostalgic view of early twentieth century life. Elmer also illustrated *The Isle of Que* by Elsie Singmaster, and a story of Johnny Appleseed for Childcraft (1948).

Usually Berta and Elmer had plans for next fall's book, but by Christmas of 1947 they were still wondering what to do. Inspiration descended on their front doorstep in the form of an astonishing snowfall. Snow was a constant problem every winter at the Hader's—that long driveway required constant shoveling in the wintertime if they were to get down to their mailbox. (When the five Carroll children who lived nearby offered to shovel the driveway up to the house, the Haders paid them five dollars, all in pennies. [222])

This time the snow was far heavier than usual. The newspapers reported that twelve inches of snow fell in a single day. It continued snowing for several days, winding up as the biggest snowstorm since the legendary blizzard of 1888. Nothing—not even trains—could move. The Haders' home on Willow Hill was completely snowed in. "The feeding stations on the ground were buried too deep to be reached by the most energetic scratching and those on the trees were heavily blanketed with snow that was turning to ice."[223] Berta and Elmer worked hard to keep their bird feeders filled and provide extra food for all the animals that inhabited or visited their property. The story about how these creatures survived in a hard winter became an obvious and natural topic for the new book.

"We put on our rose-colored spectacles and forgot all about blistered hands and aching backs in the beauty of the winter landscape . . . the models and the background for the pictures were right outside our windows." The book was completed with ease, and the animals were drawn with the delightful attention to detail that marked all Hader books. The full-color illustrations show a beautiful countryside, but the black and white pages emphasize the many little details in a winter landscape. One two-page spread shows a variety of snowflake patterns. A child could look at the book over and over again, each time spotting something new.[224]

Preliminary indications suggested *The Big Snow* might be a big seller as well. Snow was now "in" as a topic: the 1948 Caldecott medal award had gone to Roger Duvoisin for his illustrations of *White Snow, Bright Snow.*

Almost every year the Haders had insisted their contract include an escalation clause; after a certain number of books were sold, the authors would earn a larger percentage of the profits. Once automatic for all books, this had to be renegotiated in every book contract from the mid-1930s on. This time when Berta and Elmer asked for the clause to be reinserted, Macmillan balked. They caved in to company pressure and the clause disappeared. Even sixty years later the book continues to sell as a winter read-aloud and children still relate to the story of the animals' plight when the snow covers every possible thing to eat. The royalties were good because the sales were good and continue on to this day.

Caldecott Medal results were usually announced in February. In February 1949, Macmillan and the Haders received the big news that the gold medal would go to *The Big Snow*. There was a *Publishers Weekly* announcement to the press immediately, a private celebration at lunch, and a large Macmillan cocktail party. Mary Margaret McBride was asked to write a profile for the 19 March issue of *Publishers Weekly* and more articles about the Haders filled the professional journals. However, even amidst all this, they produced two more books that same year.

Berta and Elmer were now working on yet another book idea gained from their trip to Wyoming. The spotted horses they had seen and sketched reminded Elmer of one he had loved on the Monterey ranch he'd visited as a child. They completed a dummy of pictures and text about the adventures of a young cowboy and his horse and sent it off to Waldo for suggestions.

He had a good many to make. For one thing there were plenty of crickets in Wyoming, but no katydids. In regard to the horses, there were differences between an Appaloosa and a leopard-spotted horse, and he thought they might have them confused. The Appaloosa was the original Nez Perce war horse, bred for its endurance and intelligence. It had a skimpy mane and tail, with spots mainly over the hip area. The mane of the leopard-spotted horse was much fuller, and it had black spots all over the body. (Later, after consultation with experts, Waldo concluded that both types were now considered to be in the Appaloosa family.)

Waldo continued his critique. The three-month-old horse given to little Ben would still be drinking milk, not eating grain. Waldo drew a sketch of the bottle rack used for orphan babies to drink from but suggested the Haders make the horse a weanling instead. It would work better with Ben being of school age, which he would have to be if he were going to be winning roping championships in another two years. If Ben is about twelve when he gets the little

Appaloosa, he would be old enough to do all the chores Elmer gave him, and at fifteen he'd be the right age to enter roping contests.

Waldo also added a lot of detail about the cowboy's boots. Every detail has a distinct safety purpose: a sharp toe is easy to pull out of a stirrup in a hurry. The cowboy rides on the instep so it is reinforced with steel. A high heel keeps the boot from slipping out. A caring dad would have insisted Ben wear that kind of boot before allowing him to ride.

All corrals and fences are built of poles. You don't practice roping around stakes in the ground—that's a good way to be yanked out of the saddle. You use bags, which can be dragged along with the rider. No bridles—the Haders should draw hackamores with nose pieces.

Horses were no longer allowed to buck—that belonged to Hollywood. So did galloping—that gait would wear a horse out in no time. In real life horses moved at a fast walk, sometimes varied by a trot. He suggested Elmer study the paintings by Frederic S. Remington and Charles M. Russell—those two artists knew how horses and bodies moved in action.

Waldo's many suggestions meant the Haders would have to rewrite the text and do most of the drawings again. They were used to revising for editors but not rewriting the entire manuscript. They must have been appalled at the work left to do. But they believed in accuracy and had asked him for suggestions, so they went back to the studio, redid the book and sent him the new dummy. They also included a foreword giving the history of the horses.

Waldo approved the new version. It was definitely worth the rewriting. Now it could be sold in the West without people laughing at it like the Hollywood films.

Patee also liked the finished book they submitted but said Macmillan salesmen really disliked the title. It would have to be changed. Nobody would know what an appaloosa was or even how to pronounce it. But Elmer and Berta stood firm, saying children liked odd words, and the word appaloosa rolled easily off the tongue. The title stayed as *Little Appaloosa*. The Haders were right—no one had a problem with it.

They were pleased when later they received a complimentary letter from a Mr. Peckinpah of the Appaloosa Horse Club in Yuba City, California. He congratulated the Haders on their fine and accurate story and said he was giving copies to the children in his family. The Haders' thank you note to him added the information that, "The little colt of our story was discovered by my brother Waldo on a ranch nearby. He was purchased by the King Parsons Ranch of Boulder. I believe he developed into a fine type of the breed and won many honors at shows."

Little Appaloosa was released that fall, about the same time the Caldecott Award ceremony for *The Big Snow* was held. In spite of Berta's dislike of big events, the ceremony went along smoothly. The long-awaited speech had humor and insight into how the Haders learned to work together and create so many stories for children. The only glitch was unnoticeable to the audience. Just before the banquet, Frederic Melcher apologized for not having the engraved medal ready for presentation and told them that they would receive a blank medal at the ceremony. "It will be sent to you when it is engraved," Melcher promised. "I am very much embarrassed to have so delayed this, but anyway we have had two good times out of this, and a third on the occasion of delivery is ahead of me." Mr. Melcher was as good as his word. The Haders eventually received their gold medal and displayed it on the fireplace wall.

CHAPTER TWELVE

A DECADE OF CHANGE

$a$fter they won the Caldecott Medal, a kindly but naïve friend suggested that perhaps it was time for Elmer to do his oil painting full time. After all, the stone house was finished, so he didn't need to keep working on that. Mary Margaret McBride, among others, knew that would never happen. The house would never be finished because "the Haders don't have a set plan. If a project doesn't work out in practice, they just tear it out and do it over in another way. They've raised the roof right off the house two or three times to my knowledge, and maybe once or twice when I wasn't look-ing."[225] In a way, it was how they had tackled many of their books including *Little Appaloosa* and *Berta and Elmer Hader's Picture Book of the States.*

The same unrealistic friend also thought that since they had won the top award in picture book art, it meant they could now relax. Instead, the award just brought more demands on their time. Reticent and work-oriented, they'd occasionally given talks at local schools and libraries, signed books at department stores, and entertained delighted editors on Willow Hill. They had even hosted a Macmillan's annual dinner for the sales people, but had never been fond of spending a great deal of time in the public eye.

But now they found themselves to be the subject of magazine articles and theses. Collectors begged for copies of books and pictures, as did many librarians and book fair sponsors. Macmillan people wanted to have autographed books, complete with the unique illustrations the Haders sometimes added, on hand for special visitors. Parents wrote for advice about their talented young writers. ("Keep your seat on the chair," advised the Haders.) Another wanted to meet the Haders and discuss her unusual ideas pertaining to the reading process and bringing up her son.

English teachers continued to assign author letters to their students, and Berta and Elmer received a goodly share. Collectors, librarians, and booksellers assumed the Haders would be delighted to visit their institutions and celebrate Book Week or whatever other promotion was going on. Berta and Elmer did their best not to disappoint. They knew that visits often inspired children to become readers, and this was very important to them, and they appreciated the good teachers they met in the process. They wrote a thank-you note to one for "her ability to release creative gifts in your pupils" after the class gave them an Easter basket filled with the students' colored pictures.

They did their best to keep up with the requests, but one librarian got a negative reply. The Haders would not be able to attend the book fair this year, they wrote, because they had donated one of their autographed copies to the library the year before without receiving any acknowledgement. Berta and Elmer believed in thank-you notes.

People still asked how they could work together so well. On the jacket flap for one book, they say again, "We have the same kind of ideas, the same feeling about children and what they love. And the style of our work is so related that we can work perfectly together."[226] They shared their pictures with those who asked, and added well-known collectors Irvin Kerlan, Edward and Elaine Kemp, and Lena Y. de Grummond to their circle of friends. It became harder and harder to save the work time needed to keep their "Hader Heaven" from turning into what Elmer sometimes described as "Hader's Hovel."[227]

They'd learned Elmer's French art professor at the Julian was right—connections were important—and usually tried to give young hopefuls a helping hand. When Toby and Ruth Carroll wrote they had met a nice young actress in England who was coming to America hoping to break into show business, the Haders set up a dinner for her. They invited Berta's nephew, Richard Horner, who had started producing plays in New York City after he got out of the service, and his actress wife, Lynne Stuart. Young Sloane Shelton had a wonderful time and subsequently made her acting debut in 1952.

Doris Patee wrote she was leaving for a business visit to Scandinavia, and Elmer replied that it would be wonderful to see Hader books in "Svenska." After all, that was his mother's native language. They were delighted that she was still including a 15% clause for the royalties, although "when waivers are required they will be given cheerfully."[228] They also signed a contract for *Squirrely*, their first Willow Hill book. Between the work needed to keep on creating wonderful picture books and the obligation they felt to respond to requests from schools, libraries and the publishing industry, their days were full. They hosted special events when asked, including spending an entire month hosting Mary Margaret McBride's radio show at their home. But the Hader home had never been an ivory tower. They usually listened to the radio while working at their easels, and the weekenders were always full of the latest news.

The lessons of the German bombing of London were not forgotten. The horrors of the atomic bombs and the mushroom clouds over the cities of Hiroshima and Nagasaki in Japan were stark reminders of what could happen to a populated city. The Soviet Union became the new enemy, and there were fears it was developing its own atomic bomb. Since the existing roads couldn't handle a mass exodus, transportation planners decided there needed to be new and better roads to the suburbs. The 1939 New York World's Fair, sponsored by General Motors, had shown spectacular futuristic highways. Those who had seen or ridden on the German Autobahn felt it was time the United States had such high-speed roads as well.

Governor Thomas E. Dewey had proposed a 535-mile "Mainline for the Empire State," which quickly became a proposed New York State Thruway, running from New York City to Buffalo. He thought the thruway, like the old Erie Canal, would bring prosperity to the state. Work had even started in 1946 near Syracuse, too far upstate to alarm Rockland County residents, and then stalled because it was still difficult to get materials.

By 1950 Dewey was ready to begin the project once again. He wanted a route that would lead from the city directly into New

York State. They tentatively decided to cross the Hudson from Westchester County on the east bank of the Hudson to Rockland County on the west side. It would have to be at least twenty-five miles from the jurisdiction of the Port of New York Authority, since that authority was unlikely to approve anything impacting the tolls collected on the George Washington Bridge.

The engineers realized the Rockland County topography was too difficult for a thruway that required low grades and easy curves in order to maintain high speeds. While preparing for D-Day, army engineers learned how to build the caissons necessary to support a cantilever span of 1,212 feet space.[229] Now the bridge across the Tappan Zee became feasible. The site increased the costs, but Governor Dewey insisted the bridge be built as close to New York City as possible. He also did not want a repeat of the earlier local opposition, so he set up a public authority to finance, plan, construct, and maintain the road. This Thruway Authority was given "preeminent legitimacy" so local governments could not dispute claims made in the public interest. The U.S. was also engaged in the Korean War, so defense was on everyone's mind. Dewey claimed this would be a defense project, to enable New York City to be evacuated in times of war. The defense need for a thruway became the central issue, rather than the bridge itself.

The residents thought the issue had been settled long ago and felt this was a sneaky way to get the bridge built. An anti-bridge day was held. A town protest meeting was called and a formal resolution condemning the bridge was sent to Bertrand D. Talley, Chairman of the Thruway Authority. The Hudson River Conservation Society sent letters to the governor. The Haders wrote letters to all the names on their former anti-bridge lists, as well as their current correspondents, exhorting them to rally against the bridge and encourage others to do the same.

Old plans for rallying the community were brought out and revised. A song, "Over the Tappan Zee," written by the music director of the Tappan Zee High School, was published in the *New York Herald Tribune*. Later it was set to music and publicly performed by the high school chorus.[230]

No matter how the locals felt about it, Dewey's new Thruway Authority took priority over local planning. Most of the residents took pride in their beautiful countryside along the Hudson and had no desire to encourage more traffic, more automobiles, or population in their backyard. A popular 1941 song, "Let's Get Away From it All," had even named Nyack as one of the getaway towns.

Thruway Chairman Talley said it would be of maximum service to all users. Citizens were told about their wonderful future after the thruway was built. Their commute into the city would be shorter and easier. County merchants were told that this new highway would bring enough business to assure their economic recovery and prosperity. (Of course, the prime users would be truckers and those who wanted a fast route across the area, not the local shoppers.[231]) Governor Dewey announced publicly that it was a great time to invest in Rockland's future. The general mood in the county was acceptance. The bridge seemed inevitable.

However, the planners were not forthcoming about the site. They suggested it was under study, and any announced route might be changed. This made it hard to rally opposition, but Grand View residents kept the pressure on. When the final plans for the bridge were made public, they showed the bridge approach would start north of Grand View, go south along the Hudson, and then turn directly east across the Tappan Zee to Tarrytown. Although some houses in Nyack and Suffern were lost, the united opposition over the years assured the little village of Grand View-on-Hudson would survive.

Construction started almost immediately and was finished in 1955. Dewey promised it would be built using the very latest equipment developed during World War II. (When the bridge needed $6.4 billion in repairs in 2009, its poor construction was blamed on shortages from the Korean War.) Few people today remember how controversial the bridge was at the time, or how hard it was to go up against its powerful backers.

However, even if the bridge was inevitable, the rest of the proposed thruway route through Grand View was not. Another fight was looming. Rumor had it that there were plans to link the New York State Thruway to the New Jersey Turnpike, with a line running through Grand View, Piermont and Sparkill.

The planners again insisted their ideas were not set. Eventually drawings were produced showing four possible routes, with one going through Grand View. Four lanes of the highway would go along the tracks of the former Erie Railroad. Once again Elmer rallied opposition. He also posted anti-thruway signs on private and school property.

Prominent backers of the Jewish Convalescent Home joined the fight. Actress Helen Hayes, politician James Farley, and historian Carl Carmer wrote letters. A woman's group was formed called Women Against the Road to Nowhere (WARNS) which distributed a newsletter called WARNINGS. Eleanor Roosevelt devoted a column to Grand View-on-Hudson's plight.[232] Berta Hader was one of a group of women and children who held a sit-in on the Erie

Railroad tracks above Willow Hill: their picture appeared prominently in the *New York Herald Tribune*.[233] Elmer started apologizing to their book editors because they were spending so much time fighting the bridge, rather than working on their sketchpads.

News of these debates made national newspapers. Eva Reeves, a South Dakota librarian, wrote the Haders in dismay—would they lose their beloved house? Berta's hand-written reply says, "We hope not. The little stone house was built to last forever. Its roots are deep and it could not be transplanted." She continues: "We feel the shores of the Hudson River should be saved from the destruction caused by such a highway. Many years ago Washington Irving tried to save the East shore of the Hudson from the Grand Central [and] . . . he lost the fight."[234]

Then the pro-bridge engineers released a statement saying that "a decision would be made on cost alone, and human value would not be taken into account."[235] That unconsidered statement, even though true, aroused indignation across the state.

The Haders, among others, were furious. "I can understand the disregard of the human elements from the engineers' point of view but I cannot believe that all human values can be disregarded as having no weight when balanced against the dollar and cents factor," Elmer wrote. People across the country as well as in New York State were furious. After all, fighting for human values was what the war had been about. Sunday afternoon, 24 October, church bells from Stony Point to Palisades tolled for one hour to protest the road. Telegrams were sent to state government officials asking for abandonment of the entire idea.

It was also election time in New York State. Averill Harriman, running for governor against Dewey, promised "to review the situation, emphasizing human values."[236] He won the election. Soon after Harriman's election, Chairman Talley resigned. His successor never made a decision nor was a report ever made or given. The proposal quietly disappeared.

Today New Jersey's Palisades Thruway runs west of the mountains, the New York Thruway goes east of the Hudson, and River Road, the main route through Grand View-on-Hudson, remains as serene as always. As Berta had said in an earlier letter to Jane Barrow, "Some goes up and some goes down, but we'll get to the bottom all safe and sound."[237]

An armistice in Korea was announced in 1955, with the division of Korea into two parts. While some soldiers stayed, most were sent home. Just as in 1919, when Elmer was mustered out, returning soldiers were marrying and looking for homes of their own.

This time, too, dream houses were hard to find. The jobs were in New York City, but the new roads made commuting back and forth much easier. Those owning vacant land were eagerly developing it, and home construction became a major industry.

During the Second World War the army had built Camp Shanks, an embarkation camp on 2,000 acres of Rockland County, home of Grand View-on-Hudson. When it was no longer needed, the camp was turned into the largest veteran student housing development in the United States, mainly for students on the G.I. Bill who were attending Columbia University. When Columbia withdrew its sponsorship in 1951, the parcels of land were sold to the state and to local developers. Rural countrysides were covered with many small houses filled with children. Fortunately, though Rockland County still felt the pressure of an increasing population, much of its land was unbuildable and remained rural.

The trouble with adding houses for the growing families was that the countryside disappeared. A 1961 Little Golden Book, *Make Way for the Thruway*, showed many huge construction machines chewing out a route for a thruway and demolishing everything in their way. But when they reach an existing little house, inhabited by a little old woman tending her beloved roses, the workers remember how their own mothers loved roses. They find another path for the road and build it there by the light of the moon. As one says, "What a bulldozer does can't be undone," and the little house is safe. Later drivers and passengers on the thruway delight in seeing the little house and bright roses looking down on them from the hill. Author Caroline Emerson and illustrator Tibor Gergely may have been inspired by the Haders, but this scenario could have taken place in almost any U.S. city.

The Haders were known for their delight in all the small animals that also made their homes on Willow Hill. Squirrels, chipmunks, raccoons, opossums, deer mice and moles shared the hill with the woodchucks and a friendly family of skunks. The wooded slope provided shelter for a variety of birds.[238] Mary Margaret mentions starlings flying in through open windows and once finding a friendly chipmunk "sitting spang in the middle of a warm blueberry pie in the kitchen." Even when some flying squirrels decided to spend the winter in the attic and made beds in Elmer's shirt drawers, they were allowed to stay.

After Mary Margaret McBride had had John Kieran, a panelist on the popular radio quiz program, *Information, Please!* on her own radio show, she learned he was also a naturalist and bird watcher. She decided to put him to the test and persuaded Berta and Elmer to go along. In *Out of the Air* she says: "One of our most delightful broadcasts was with John [Kieran] high on a hill on the front terrace of the Haders home on the Hudson. The birds were singing fit to burst their throats and John identified each in turn. We broadcast from Hader House for a whole month that summer and were enchanted with the rosy dawns, golden sunsets, and companionship of birds and animals."[239]

Some orphaned animals actually lived in the Haders' house. Mary Margaret had to share her guest room once with a little gray squirrel, who Berta had rescued. Now these animals took center stage in several books set on Willow Hill. The first one, *Squirrely of Willow Hill,* was published in 1950. Eventually, he grew too big to be confined, and the Haders took him to a refuge on nearby Bear Mountain Park. To their great delight, when they visited him at the park, he would run down a tree to greet them.

His remembered antics made Squirrely the perfect candidate for a picture book bearing his name. In the book Berta and Elmer thinly disguised themselves as the householders, Mr. and Mrs. McGinty, who turn a nail keg into a little hanging nest and bring leaves into the room so Squirrely can hide his acorns. Even though Squirrely was no longer on Willow Hill, Elmer wrote Doris that they still had three frisky squirrels they could sketch from their living room windows. *Lost in the Zoo* (1951), their next book, was based on a newspaper story, and gave them a chance to go back to the zoo and draw animals, including those African animals they had illustrated for Hamilton Williamson's stories.

They returned to Willow Hill for *Little Whitefoot: His Adventures on Willow Hill* (1952). The little stone house provided many opportunities for field mice to come in out of the cold. Berta's system for dealing with them was to put a thimbleful of peanut butter on a piece of cardboard. A glass bowl covered the cardboard with a thimble propping it up on one side. When the mouse scampered under for the peanut butter, the bowl would fall, safely trapping it inside. The next morning Berta or Elmer would carefully take the bowl and cardboard outside and release the occupant. They learned much about the wild mice around them and used much of this information in the book, but the story is really about some clothed and humanlike mice who live inside a dollhouse in the attic. Patee never liked anthropomorphic animals, but the pictures were enchanting.

The next Willow Hill book, *Wish on the Moon*, also had the animals behaving in humanlike ways. Some of the animals on the hill overhear Mrs. McGinty wishing for a beautiful garden, and they also know that wishing on a certain special moon will make wishes come true. So they get the animals together on the special night, all wish for the garden at once, and indeed Mrs. McGinty sees a glorious garden flowering all around her when the next spring arrives. As usual, every little animal seems to have a distinct personality.

The Friendly Phoebe, like Squirrely of *Willow Hill*, was based on another little orphan, a phoebe, they adopted and raised until it could live independently. Berta rescued it from under a tree, and both Haders took on the role of parenting, which meant feeding the baby with medicine every twenty minutes or so during daylight hours. Berta concocted some food while it was little, and then Elmer took on the task of catching insects for it until they could teach it to catch them for itself. They believed all wild animals belonged in the wild, so they worked hard at teaching it survival skills such as how to eat and how to fly. Even when it finally went off during the day, it kept flying through the window and perching on the lamps every night. They eventually had to put up window screens.

The idea for the next Willow Hill book, *The Runaways, a Tale of the Woodlands* (1956), came out of their real life experiences with suburban development taking over the habitat that used to belong to the animals. In this book the animals being forced from their usual places discover the railroad tracks as the only safe place away from the bulldozers. Then, just below the tracks, they find the McGintys' animal haven. The last one in this series, *Little Chip of Willow Hill* (1958), was based on the chipmunks that roamed their property.

In 1958 President Dwight D. Eisenhower signed the Alaska Statehood Act which made Alaska the 49th state in January 1959. That reminded the Haders of an interesting story they'd discovered when researching for *Chuck-a-luck and His Reindeer*. They had learned that reindeer are NOT native to Alaska, in spite of the common belief of them always having lived at the North Pole with Santa Claus. Many Native Alaskans were short of food because of massive hunting and fishing by outsiders, and they needed a dependable food supply. Since the native caribou could not be herded, the U.S. government sponsored importing the caribou-like reindeer from Lapland to Alaska. The government also encouraged many Laplanders to immigrate along with their animals and teach Alaskans how to manage the herds. The reindeer were brought across the Atlantic Ocean to New York, across the United States to Seattle, and then loaded on ships again for the final leg of the voyage to Alaska. The Laplanders took such good care of the animals that only one was lost during that entire trip. It was a great story with pictures showing colorful Laplanders and reindeer arriving in Alaska, where a Laplander boy and an Eskimo boy become friends. *Reindeer Trail: A Long Journey from Lapland to America* debuted in 1959, not long after Alaska's statehood. It was a wonderful book. The timing was great, and it gave children a new glimpse into both different animals and different cultures.

The two nature stories that followed are very similar to the Willow Hill books. One, *Mr. Billy's Gun* (1960), uses Berta's mother Adelaide and her husband Billy Gordon as characters and models for the illustrations. Mr. Billy doesn't like the birds feeding in his garden, and when he finds that scarecrows don't work, he decides shooting the birds will be the only solution. However, once he is laid up in bed with a broken leg, he discovers the joy of watching them out his window. *Quack Quack: the Story of a Little Wild Duck* (1961) was also based on the wildlife near Willow Hill and makes the readers think how wonderful it would be to be able to fly away.

Then two more books came out of that long ago trip to Lander, Wyoming. *Home On The Range: Jeremiah Jones and His Friend Little Bear in the Wild* West was published in 1955. Jerry can't wait for summer when he'll be a real cowboy on his grandparent's ranch. However, when the long awaited trip happens, Jerry discovers he still has a lot of boring indoor chores to do. Little Bear thinks life on the ranch would be much easier. So the two boys decide to trade places. Jerry goes off to the Indian camp where a Pow Wow is held to celebrate his adoption into Little Bear's tribe. Little Bear takes his place on the ranch. After the excitement of the Pow Wow is over, Jerry is homesick and decides to return to his grandparents. As he gets on the trail to the ranch, he meets Little Bear who is also heading home. The book ends with the message: "Everybody was happy in his own home on the range."

Doris Patee didn't like the sketches of Jerry—they weren't nearly as good as those of Ben in *Little Appaloosa*. She also suggested that the Appaloosa wasn't quite right, stating, "You do a better job with squirrels." However, Berta and Elmer came up with versions that matched what Patee had in mind. This 1962 book was the last one that they all worked on together. More changes were coming.

CHAPTER THIRTEEN

CHANGES IN PUBLISHING

The Cold War also influenced the publishing world. Large numbers of children, soon to be referred to as the "Baby Boomers," had arrived en masse in the public schools during the 1950s. Unlike earlier generations, these children now had more worldly and educated parents, thanks to the G. I. Bill and the fact that many of their mothers had previously been employed outside the home. They had seen different ways of making a living in the world and wanted their children to have the very best educational opportunities possible. Most of all, they expected them to learn to read.

During the thirties and forties, children had generally learned by "sight reading," recognizing whole words (but not analyzing them) as they appeared in print. One of the proponents of this method, Edward William Dolch, prepared a list of the 225 words most commonly found in those times which were used in the basic school readers. Learning whole words worked for some children, but many still struggled with reading, especially outside of school texts.

In May 1954, *Life* magazine published a report on illiteracy among school children, concluding that children were not learning to read because their books were boring. Many new words had been added to the vocabulary of post-war America, and the new emphasis on science made it worse. The new discoveries about dinosaurs and space flight were exciting, but if you didn't know how to sound out a word, they were impossible to read. Rudolf Flesch wrote *Why Johnny Can't Read: And What You Can Do About It* in 1955. He advocated reviving the phonics method, where readers could learn how to sound out the words they didn't know.

William Ellsworth Spaulding of Houghton Mifflin tackled the boring aspect by asking the very popular Theodore Geisel (a.k.a. Dr. Seuss) to write a book using only 385 simple and recognizable words—but the book also had to be one that a child couldn't put down. Geisel struggled over the challenge, but eventually met it with *The Cat in the Hat* in 1957. His inevitable rhymes and fantastic illustrations appealed to parents and children. The books were so popular that Random House set up the *Beginner Books* with an easily seen *Cat in the Hat* logo. The same year Harper inaugurated the *I Can Read* series with Else Minarik's *Little Bear* illustrated by Maurice Sendak and *Danny and the Dinosaur* illustrated by Syd Hoff. All three had a cartoon-like dynamic style.

When the Soviet Union launched the satellite *Sputnik* in 1957, the United States was stunned. Many felt the U.S. was falling behind Russia in preparing children for the future. The National Defense Education Act (NDEA) was passed quickly by Congress to bring U.S. schools up to speed, and President Eisenhower signed it into law in September 1958, providing funding to United States education institutions at all levels, including elementary schools.

In April 1961, an article entitled "Is Your Child a Victim of the Library Gap?" appeared in *This Week* magazine, a Sunday supplement in many American newspapers. Not only did it call attention to the importance of good school libraries and trained librarians in the schools, it also suggested readers could take action by writing to the American Library Association in care of the newspaper for a free booklet about school libraries.[240] The article also inspired the directors of the Knapp Foundation of North Carolina to appropriate over a million dollars to set up school library demonstration projects throughout the country.

This Knapp School Libraries Project, under the direction of Peggy Sullivan, showed clearly how school libraries improved both teaching and learning. The Elementary and Secondary Education Act of 1963 also supported the training of specialized school librarians and the establishment of school library media centers— named such because of the realization that audio-visual media complemented the printed book.[241]

These school librarians learned how to choose books of quality and match them with the interests of children, the needs of teachers, and the requirements of various curriculums. Publishers lost little time in catering to this new educational market, and many brand new science and social studies books arrived in schools across the nation. When the Haders began writing, there were only sixty or seventy children's books published each fall. By 1963 there were nearly 3,000.

The Haders' emphasis on nature fit very nicely into the new emphasis on science. Teachers enjoyed incorporating the Willow

Hill books into their nature study because children could learn to pay attention to the natural world around them. *The Big Snow*, of course, was a very popular read-aloud, not only because it had been a Caldecott winner, but because it became current every winter in the north part of the country. The stories showed how humans and animals could interact helpfully.

In the Hader books text and pictures depend on each other, and their detailed illustrations provide background to the story. Since color printing had been very expensive, few books were printed with full-color illustrations. The Hader illustrations could work well in color and in black and white.

Then, in 1963, Maurice Sendak's *Where the Wild Things Are* was published, and the modern era in children's books began. Almost immediately, books full of color illustrations were all around them, and the illustrations became more important than the texts. In a letter to Marion Webb, the Haders speak of many recent books seemingly influenced by the comic pages.[242] Colorful books had instant appeal.

In her succinct summary of picture books, Mary Milham Burns points out how "seductively elaborate art overwhelms story or distracts readers from weak texts," how "various critics have expressed concern about a tendency to celebrate showmanship over substance," and how, "at the beginning of the twenty-first century, we may be in danger of confusing gilt with gold, when we should be asking whether or not the emperor is wearing clothes."[243]

Burns was right. Subsequent picture books have wonderful illustrations that add much to a child's ability to appreciate art. However, often these visuals do distract from today's limited amount of text. Modern picture books require less reading of text and less imagination from their readers. Publishers were carrying out Berta's early observation "Illustration beats explanation."

All of these trends were impacting publishing. Other trends, often unseen by workers in the industry, were going on at the executive level. Until the sixties, most of the influential publishers were wealthy gentlemen who enjoyed the prestige of being involved in an admired business, and were satisfied with a modest profit. Making money was not as important as bringing out excellent books that were well-reviewed, appreciated in themselves, and seen as having lasting value. These men—and they were all men then—could and did take their time, hiring good editors who could spot future talent and develop authors to an admired and often profitable status. But in the late sixties, these influential executives were dying off. Their heirs often could not afford the inheritance taxes and sold off the company. The new company then had to pay off the debt involved in the acquisition. The financial side of the publishing firm began to be involved in editorial decisions, and many long time editors left for other venues.

In one of her journal articles, Louise Seaman Bechtel quoted a letter about publishers written by a George Withers in 1625.

> An honest stationer or publisher is he who exercises his craft (whether it be in printing, binding, or selling of books) with more respect to the glory of God and the public advantage than to his own commodity and is both an ornament and a profitable member to the civil commonwealth. If he be a printer, he copies fairly and truly. If he is a bookbinder, he is no mere bookseller who sells ink and paper bundled up together merely for his own advantage, but he is a retailer of knowledge, of wisdom, and of much experience for little money.

> The reputation of scholars is as dear to him as his own: for he acknowledges that they both begin and continue supporting his craft. He heartily loves and seeks the prosperity of his own corporation, but would not injure the universities to advantage it. In a word, he is such a man that the state ought to cherish him, scholars to love him, good customers to frequent his shop, and the whole company of stationers to pray for him.[244]

These were not the companies of the 1960s. Now publishing corporations needed to maximize profits, and the goal changed from bringing out the very best products to those that could sell best and be produced more cheaply.

Berta and Elmer, who had enjoyed over thirty years of good professional and personal relationships with Seaman and Patee, now found themselves dealing with a changing slate of editors. Long time editor Doris Patee retired from Macmillan in 1959. She was replaced by Lee Anna Diedrick and then Frances Keene in 1964. Keene didn't last long: Susan Hirschman left Harpers and moved to Macmillan, taking over the editor's desk in the fall of that same year.

Although Hirschman had loved the Hader books when she was a child, she knew their books no longer met the demands of the contemporary book market. They were longer than most of the recent picture books, and their artistic style seemed dated. She also had definite reservations about their book proposals. Two were based on history, but not fully focused on the subject. She felt their dummy for "High Tor, a Hudson River History" had possibilities as a history but did not like the travelogue aspects. It needed rewriting for the elementary school market. She turned down "A Crown for Powhatan" for similar reasons: the Haders had woven a story around a relatively unknown and unverified topic, that the King of England sent a gold crown to Powhatan who refused it—and she didn't feel "the combination of story and history" would sell very well. The one book she accepted met with several publishing delays. *Two Is Company, Three's a Crowd* came out in 1967 as the Haders' first spring book. It was an appropriate time for a book about wild geese, but all previous books had been planned for November's Book Week and the Christmas market.

Macmillan celebrated its fiftieth anniversary in 1969. In response to a letter from Hirschman, the Haders pointed out that they had published over forty-five books with the company, "and we expect to add many more." They did not realize that they had published their last children's book, though they still received royalties from the backlist of their previous books.

Berta, normally the sunny optimist, wrote the following note in her 1967 travel journal. There was no explanation, just the phrase "Organizations become more complex as they expand until they kill themselves." It probably was something she heard on the radio, but it shows how aware she had become of the changing world.

Hoping to boost profits, Macmillan began acquiring companies outside of the publishing business. When these investments soured during the 1974 recession, Macmillan drastically cut its publishing staff. Susan Hirschman, the Haders' last editor, resigned and started the Greenwillow imprint at William Morrow. Most of her staff and authors followed her. In a response to a letter from Berta, she agreed that the "real Macmillan—Louise Seaman's and Doris Patee's Macmillan"—was no more. Only the name remained.[245]

At one time publishers also could be sure that a good author would last over the decades. "Backlist" books had earned back all their costs of production, and now became a profitable part of the business. That, too, changed in 1979 when the Supreme Court decided a case in favor of the Internal Revenue Service against the Thor Tool Company.

Until then, whatever tool Thor produced but could not sell had been thought to lose value as it sat in a warehouse. This let the tool companies write off these "losses" against their income. The Thor decision stated these inventories still had their original value, meaning the company lost its deduction and paid more taxes. As applied to publishing, it made it more expensive to carry inventory from year to year.[246]

After Thor, there was little interest in backlists. The older ones were now a tax liability and couldn't afford to be kept in storage for the future. When a first printing of books was sold out, they were rarely reprinted, with the exception of award winners, books that publishers could promote as modern classics, such as *Good Night, Moon*, or those that could be packaged in educational sets for schools. Older authors, even those who had been as popular as the Haders once had been, were now forgotten. It was left to librarians to preserve their legacy for future generations. As one university administrator of manuscripts put it, "The primary function of a university is to transmit the knowledge of the past to students in order for them to solve the problems of the future."[247] Until the recent communication revolution, most of this knowledge was transmitted to children through literature.

→ CHAPTER FOURTEEN ←

TOGETHER FOREVER: THEIR LEGACY

God made all the creatures and gave them
our love and fear.

To give sign we're all God's children, one big
family here.

—Robert Browning[248]

This quote, remembered from my own girlhood, seems to sum up the myriad legacies left behind after Elmer and Berta passed away—he in 1973 and she in 1976. In an article about the Haders in the *Instructor* of November, 1951 author E. F. Noonan reported that Berta told their life story in one sentence: "Elmer and I were married in 1919 and we have lived happily ever since."

Even when the Haders were no longer working on books, the little stone house continued to keep them busy. Berta wrote Jane about the occasional downpours causing streams of water in the cellar. "We just leave the cellar door open and it runs out." [249] However, they did have to hire people to handle the ever-troublesome roof and gutters.

It can't have been easy to adjust to a life without deadlines, but it meant they could visit friends without guilt, and Berta could visit any friend who needed her. Their nephew Richard Horner was now a play producer with an actress wife, and they often went to New York to visit him and go to well-known and not-so-well-known plays. They could get tickets to almost any play around.

They often traveled: short trips to visit Doris Patee at her summer shore retreat in Quonochontaug, Rhode Island, more popularly referred to as "Quon." They thoroughly enjoyed visiting Mary Margaret McBride's and Stella Karn's homes in Shokan, New York, and the countryside around there inspired many of Elmer's later paintings. They took a trip west to the new Wilder museum in DeSmet, North Dakota, and delivered a handmade quilt that Rose had made for Berta. When they visited Mansfield, Missouri they were surprised to see Elmer's old painting of Telegraph Hill hanging over the fireplace in the Mansfield house. [250]

There were fewer of the long-term weekenders around the big chestnut table, but visitors still continued to travel to the fairy-tale house on Willow Hill. Widowed Mary Parton often came by with her daughter Margaret. Berta still delighted in preparing food, and Elmer's ability to be a good host had not abated. On pleasant days, visitors and the Haders usually ate lunch on the front terrace with a view of the river and the mulberry trees with the wren nests. The breezes were fragrant with the scents of the surrounding gardens.

A 1934 article in the Nyack *Journal* told of a homebound commuter on the Northern Branch of the Erie Railroad who, sitting on the river side of the *Flyer,* was looking down on the low and spreading green-roofed and gabled house of red-brown stone. "It makes you think of the pictures of Wordsworth's cottage you used to see when you were studying the English poets in school," she remarked. "If I ever have a home that's the sort of home I would like to have."

"That's Berta and Elmer Haders' home," the other traveler answered. "They're artists. Maybe that's why it's so nice."[251]

Being artists undoubtedly meant they recognized the charms of the old Dutch houses surrounding them, and why they chose to build one of their own. It meant they had an eye towards the most artistic placement of windows and doors. Their love of nature ensured that they did as little damage as possible to their lot, leaving plenty of wooded areas where small animals could hide. Their appreciation of the riotous colors of flowers meant being surrounded by them most of the year, many provided by friends who couldn't resist sharing their own garden specialties.

What those commuters couldn't see was how nice the house was inside. The furnishings inside were arranged by an artist's eye, but they reflected the Haders' whole-hearted gift of friendship, welcome, and uncritical love. They came from a vast range of places inhabited or traveled to by friends. Bessie Beatty had brought Berta a little doll handmade of moss and pinecones when she returned from her Russian stint with the women's "Battalion of Death." Berta cherished it because of its character and because "it seems to be completely from the forest."[252] Braided straw rugs from Central America, Mexican tables, and a Chinese sewing basket sat comfortably together, mute reminders of various people who'd enjoyed the Haders' hospitality over the years.[253] Elmer's grand piano stood in one corner, facing the painting he had done of Berta before their marriage.

The same *Instructor* article reported, "Everything that our eyes fell upon bespoke an individual charm achieved by those who create. . . . I wondered if it was the same talent that designed the house, created the books, cooked the food and shingled the roof. I decided that it was—a fused talent of two persons who decided what they wanted to achieve and are realizing it."[254] She was right.

The house still sits on the hill looking over the Tappan Zee, as quaint as any cottage in a fairy tale. It is a legacy that is a visible reminder of two residents who helped keep Grand View-on-Hudson so charming. As it aged it needed extensive repairs, almost to the point of replacement—no wonder, considering the original builders' experience!—but the present owner remembered admiring the house when he was a little boy riding past it on his bike. He restored it as much as possible to its former glory, though said it was impossible to replicate all the little flower niches and birdhouses built into the original walls. If houses keep their original atmospheres, this one must surround the occupants with welcoming warmth and charm and love.

And the Haders left behind many small private acts of kindness. Mary Margaret McBride said that if anyone had problems, Berta would visit and just listen to them. Ernestine Evans mentions how hard it was to keep contact with Elsie Weil in her later years, when she had lost much of her memory. Berta could—and did.

Another legacy is their passion and appreciation of surroundings, from the mountains to the rivers and more. "All through the years we have enjoyed making picture books for children and we always hope the world they inherit will be as beautiful as our world has been."[255] They joined many national conservation organizations from Save-the-Redwoods to Defenders of Wildlife. Elmer was on the board of the Hudson River Conservation Society for much of his life, and was very pleased with President Lyndon Johnson's emphasis on preserving "the natural beauty[256] and historical areas of our country." Readers could identify with the animals and children in their stories, and many grew up interested in conserving their environment. The Haders replied to one teacher that their books were *not* written as a "plea to be kind to animals." They were written to encourage children to appreciate their surroundings. They taught by example, not by preaching.

Berta was with Elmer as he slowly slipped away. He died peacefully in his sleep in 1973 at a Rockland County hospital near his beloved home on Willow Hill.

"What are you thinking, Darling?" asked Berta who was sitting with him in the hospital room.

"I'm thinking I was damn lucky," he replied. Those were his last words. And so he had been. But he'd worked hard to create his own luck, from the days of the San Francisco earthquake in 1906 to the end of his life. He'd recognized what he wanted, worked hard to get it, and adapted to whatever circumstances were necessary. If one way didn't work out, he'd find another. Jerome Kern's Depression era song must have run through his mind often for he certainly believed in picking himself up and starting all over again.

In recent years there has been quite an interest in the "pursuit of happiness." Academics have written about it, there have been television shows, and there even was a happiness conference in far-away Bhutan, a country that maintains a happiness index in contrast to the more usual economic indexes. If people were rated on the happiness index, surely the Haders would have been near the top. When Mary Margaret McBride interviewed them near their fiftieth wedding anniversary, she asked them about their secret to having a happy marriage. Berta didn't hesitate. "Marry someone who likes the same things you do," she said. She and Elmer both did. The word "fused talents" used by the *Instructor* writer was a perfect description of their entire lives.

Berta continued in their home, enjoying her flowers and the wildlife, and keeping up her correspondence with friends. Most of the people who knew and loved and worked with the Haders were gone, but Margaret Parton, Lem, and Mary's daughter whom Berta had babysat in San Francisco, lived nearby. She continued to see Berta and Elmer until the end of their lives.

When Edward and Elaine Kemp, two librarians from the University of Oregon, came by, interested in the entire process of how children's books were created, the Haders were happy to share their memories as well as to begin emptying the attic. As each of their books had been finished, Berta had carefully wrapped up all the materials used in its production—notes on scrap paper, sketches, jottings on envelopes, dummies, and a copy of the finished book—into a carefully tied package and stored it there. Berta and Elmer were so pleased with the appreciation for their work that the Kemps showed, that they eventually donated forty-some boxes of material to the University of Oregon Special Collections. Most of the remaining materials, inherited by niece Joy Rich, were given to Concordia University in Portland, Oregon, for a permanent exhibit.

Berta lived on until 1976 'in the little stone house,' finding comfort in the knowledge that they had accomplished the two things they most wanted to do. They preserved, unspoiled, their lovely woodland corner, a sanctuary for birds and wild life. And they wrote and illustrated books which children love and remember, books which make them aware of the appeal of animals and the beauty of nature everywhere.[257]

She continued to maintain their home, feed their animal friends, and keep in touch with their human ones, even though she was often short of breath and felt tired. She was anxious to finish cleaning out the attic, too. She wrote Jane Barrow that she was readying a load of drawings for Mr. Kemp. "I got up early and I expect to work late—if I ever do all I plan to do I will be ready for cloud nine . . .. I live by the motto 'Live as tho immortal to the last mortal breath.' That's the way it was with Elmer, for he never seemed to worry about himself and I am so glad. He was always so gentle and patient and darling."

Berta kept up their Christmas card tradition through 1975. When she discovered that she had terminal cancer, she spent her last few weeks with nephew Richard and his wife Lynne in their Manhattan home. As she was dying, she told friends that Richard and Lynne made her so comfortable that "I feel I've died and am already in heaven." The last Hader Christmas card (1975) depicts her as an angel floating serenely among the stars over Willow Hill where her ashes and Elmer's join under one of the willow trees near their beloved little stone house.[258]

Richard inherited the house with its furnishings, paintings, and manuscripts. Hopeful that Berta and Elmer not be forgotten, he and Lynne republished some of the early picture books. They also hoped to create a television show about their lives and wrote to as many of the surviving Hader friends as possible, asking for memories and anecdotes. Many responded with stories and accounts of happy times spent on Willow Hill.

When people refer to the "Golden Age of Publishing" they are referring to the days when quality was considered all-important. Berta and Elmer and their editors were all doing their best to achieve wonderful books for children. When once asked why they wrote for children, they replied that

> We write illustrated books for children in the hope that stories and pictures will:
>
> 1. Interest and amuse young readers
>
> 2. Awaken and cultivate a kindly feeling toward other children as well as the birds and domestic animals about the house and the gentle creatures of field and forest who share the world they live in.
>
> 3. We write for children, not to preach, nor moralize, but to suggest that the world about them is a beautiful and pleasant place to live in, if they take time out to look. And perhaps in so doing, our young readers will develop an interest to save what is good of their world for others to enjoy.[259]

They didn't write for glory, but they touched many lives. Their books are their legacy. Many children who grew up in the twentieth century remember Hader books as part of their childhood. These readers learned that other children and animals might live varied lives in different places but have the same feelings as everyone else. The Hader illustrations provided realistic backgrounds that enhanced this message.

The Haders were extremely generous to those who were interested in their work. They sent art and artifacts to Dr. Lena Y. de Grummond when she decided to establish a research collection at the University of Southern Mississippi. They did the same for Dr. Irvin Kerlan whose collection is now at the University of Minnesota. Some works can be found in Wichita, Kansas, and at the May Massee collection in the Emporia State University archives.

In a "Letter to the Editor" written to the *South of the Mountains* publication of the Rockland Historical Society, a young woman remembered a snowy Christmas shortly after *The Big Snow* came out. She—a total stranger—had called to ask if the Haders would autograph a copy of the book for the children of a favorite Michigan college professor. They invited her out; she "climbed the slippery, icy, steps, tapped on the door, and was ushered into a fairyland." She never forgot the magic, and many years later the professor told her his children still treasured the book. She ended her letter with the words: "Such simple acts of gentleness and courtesy always come back and bless others."[260]

A fine legacy indeed.

ACKNOWLEDGEMENTS

Culch is an old-fashioned New England word for things that are saved because they might be useful in the future. A culch drawer might have string or postage stamps, photos or letters. This biography could never have been written without the savers who kept the "culch" about Berta and Elmer Hader over the years, knowing that someday it would be needed.

Saver number one was Berta Hoerner Hader. She kept letters from their friends, odd sketches and jottings, and their own writings whether for publication or for themselves. When a book was finished, she carefully wrapped up everything that related to the project, including dummies, notes, and correspondence, and stored the materials in their attic.

When Edward and Elaine Kemp, librarians from the University of Oregon, began collecting materials from outstanding children's authors and illustrators to be added to the university's collection about the creation of children's literature, they visited the Haders. Berta and

Elmer agreed to give many of their stored manuscripts and art to the University of Oregon where it would be housed safely and well. Each time the Kemps came calling, they left with a great deal of invaluable material and warm memories of two wonderful friends.

Librarians create ordered collections from saved culch. Back at the University of Oregon, the materials were carefully labeled, packed in archival material, and cataloged so future students could study them. Special Collections librarians James Fox, Bruce Tabb, and Linda Long generously shared this collection and their expertise with me, as did the Kemps who had originally collected the material. I owe much to librarians Brian Jennings at the New City N.Y. Library, Jim Carmin at the Multnomah County Library, Ruth Murray at Portland State University, and to the librarians at the Douglas County Library System in Roseburg, Oregon, the San Francisco Public Library, the New York Public Library, and the Nyack N.Y. Library. Thanks also to Richard Kielbowicz of the University of Washington and Steve Kochersperger, the U.S. Postal Service's Senior Research Analyst, for their extensive research into the pertinent postal regulations. They unearthed the reason behind the magazine publishers' decisions to drop children's pages in the 1920s.

Staff at the Herbert Hoover Library in Iowa answered questions about Rose Wilder Lane, a close friend of Berta's in the early days. Toby Himmel of the School of Ethical Culture in New York City provided information about Berta's time there, and the University of Washington sent Berta's college transcript.

Other savers who made this book possible were Joy's brother and sister-in-law, Richard Horner and Lynne Stuart, who had inherited the house on Willow Hill. Not only did they preserve much of the material remaining in the house, they also wrote to the weekenders and other friends not long after the Haders passed away, asking for memories of the times spent with Berta and Elmer. They kept the replies they received, as well as Elmer's journal and manuscripts about the building of the Haders' handcrafted house. Unattributed quotations in chapters 3, 4, and 5 about Willow Hill are in Elmer's own words. Rich inherited these materials after her brother's death.

Another saver was the new owner of the Haders' home on Willow Hill. The Haders and their friends had worked hard when building the house in the 1920s, but ninety years later it needed extensive renovation. When a worker fell through the roof into an unknown room filled with art, many builders would have tossed the room's contents into the nearest dumpster. Instead, Mark Goldstein packed up all the contents from that hidden room, and kept them in a dark, dry space hoping one day to get in touch with the original owners. When Joy Hoerner Rich showed up on an unexpected visit, he gave her all those saved materials.

Although Joy had been preserving family books, art, and letters, these new collections were overwhelming. She set up a nonprofit organization, *Hader Connection*, to protect it and chose Karen Tolley, a knowledgeable book person, to direct it. This book also owes much to the support of the *Hader Connection* board of directors: Kerwin Doughton, William Duncan, Ann Kjensrud, Lenore Paulsen, Joan Seitz, Rebecca Sorensen, Mary Sykes, Marilyn Woodrich, and John Waller. Besides developing educational exhibits and an art curriculum, the group also encouraged the production of a book showcasing the varied Hader art with the help of another team of artists, John and Judy Waller. *Berta and Elmer*

Hader: a Lifetime of Art was published in 2013. It includes nearly 300 images, leaving little room for mentioning much about the Haders' many other lifetime contributions to children's literature and their community. This book fills in those gaps.

The Haders not only cultivated their friends at Willow Hill, they also kept up a correspondence with friends and family who lived far away. Many of these valued the letters and sketches they received and passed them on to libraries at their own favorite institutions. Librarians Dean Rogers at Vassar College, Rita Smith at the University of Florida, and Ellen Ruffin at the University of Southern Mississippi all shared their collections of letters. Since the Haders were colorful writers as well as artists, wherever possible I have quoted directly from the various letters in these files.

Bill Lee, whose mother was a close friend and neighbor of the Haders, shared his own memoir and photographs of the Haders. Evelyn Polesny, owner and proprietor of the house on 31 Jones Street in Greenwich Village, New York, welcomed us into her home—the same old house that Berta and Rose Wilder Lane rented and shared with so many friends in 1918-1919. Polesny and her husband have turned the house into the Jones Street Guest House (with heat!) where one can stay and feel a part of twentieth century Greenwich Village.

Besides all the other people who patiently answered questions by phone or in writing and also to those who encouraged the book's development and/or proofed the manuscript: Leonard Marcus, Karen Tolley, Samantha Waltz, Jennifer Margulis, and Mary Ellen Marmaduke. I also want to thank John and Judy Waller and Yvonne Branchflower for answering my many art questions. Thanks also go to my family for putting up with my frequent abstractedness and to Josh Chapman for coming up with the perfect title.

Many thanks go to Edward and Elaine Kemp, librarians at the University of Oregon, for making friends with the Haders and persuading them to donate a large proportion of their original creations to the university. The Kemps willingly shared their notes and personal remembrances with me.

My eternal gratitude goes to Concordia University, especially Brent Mai, Linda Church, Greg Lewis, and Katherine Dunbar, for their support of a book about two examples of the "Golden Age of Publishing."

S.A.C.

Endnotes

1   He was hindered by the fact that Joy's brother had earlier changed the spelling of his surname from Hoerner to Horner.

2   Lane (1917), jacket.

3   Dillon (1985).

4   Dillon (1985).

5   Beman (1989a), pp. 113-118.

6   Ibid., p. 70, lists Mrs. Harry Lafler as the subject of Hader's "En Kimono" exhibited in the 1918 Bohemian Club display at the Palace of Fine Arts, 22 March to 22 May 1918.

7   Hader, Elmer Stanley (1917).

8   Lane (1917).

9   This verse appeared earlier in *Sunset Magazine*, Southern Pacific Co. Passenger Department, vol. 13, 1904, while the author was still at Stanford. Irwin became a well-known New York City journalist, who wrote an article about San Francisco, "The City that Was," while the city was in flames. The poem was later quoted in *Laughter on the Hill* by Margaret Parton.

10   McBride (1969).

11   Hader, Elmer Stanley (1947).

12   McBride (1969).

13   Bessie Beatty was usually called "Betty" by her friends but used Bessie professionally.

14   Wilder (1974), p. 52.

15   Ibid., p. 66.

16   McBride (1969).

17   University of Oregon. Letter from Rose Wilder Lane to Berta & Elmer dated 25 November 1925.

18   The word "Bohemian" refers to journalists, and this private gentleman's club was originally founded by in 1872 by reporters at the *San Francisco Chronicle.* This was a club for journalists (full members) and artists and writers (honorary members). The club evolved over the years into a group of businessmen and politicians. Will Irwin's memoir, *The Making of a Reporter* (Putnam, 1942), mentions the purchase of the Bohemian Grove in the early 1900s. It was a casual place where members partied and put on plays. Jack London and Bret Harte were early members. Source: "Bohemian Club," Wikipedia and Irwin's memoir. *The Making of a Reporter.*

19   Soon absorbed by Watsonville, California: Elmer counted himself as a native San Franciscan.

20   University of Oregon. Letter from Berta to Ada Randall, teacher, responding to questions.

21   Hopkins (1969), p. 149.

22   University of Oregon. Letter from Elmer to Mary Margaret McBride.

23   Griffis (1929), p. 13.

24   University of Oregon. Berta Hoerner Hader's Gordon letters.

25   Concordia University. Letter from Adelaide Jennings Hoerner to Berta dated 3 November 1940.

26   Concordia University. Letter from Adelaide Jennings Hoerner to Berta dated May 1921.

27   Kemp (1977).

28   Concordia University. Letter from Adelaide Jennings to Berta dated 3 November 1940.

29   Hopkins (1969), p. 148.

30   Beman (1989a), p. 10.

31   Russell (1989).

32   Beman (1989a).

33   Horner & Stuart (1981).

34   Letter to Sybilla A. Cook from Toby Himmel, Director of Alumni Relations, Ethical Culture Fieldston School, Bronx, New York.

35   Kemp (1977).

36   University of Oregon. Night Lettergram to Elmer at New York General Delivery.

37   University of Oregon. Letter from Waldo Hader to Elmer.

38   Kemp (2009a).

39   Beman (1989a), p. 15.

40   Jean Stern, Director of the Irvine Museum, California. "History of Plein Air Art." (http://www.crystalcovebeachcottages.com/resources/) – accessed in 2012.

41   University of Oregon. Elmer's painting license.

42   McBride (1969).

43   University of Washington. Academic Transcript of Berta Hoerner.

44   Kemp (2009b).

45   McBride (1969).

46   *San Francisco Bulletin,* 16 March 1918.

47   Beman (1989a), p. 17.

48   University of Oregon.

49   Taber (1917).

50   Hader, Elmer (1917), p. 12.

51   Lane (1917).

52   Beman (1989a), p. 20.

53   Connelly (1972), p. 7.

54   University of Oregon.

55   The woman who formed the unit felt the men were not fighting hard enough.

56   McBride (1969).

57   Bodin (1918).

58   McBride (1969).

59   Adickes (1991), p. 4.

60   Ibid., p. 32.

61   Sochen (1972), p. 3.

62   Adickes (1991), p. 32.

63   University of Oregon. Letter from Rose Wilder Lane about some old friends, including the Haders, circa 1935.

64   Holtz (1991).

65   Holtz (1991). Concordia University. Letter from Rose Wilder Lane to Dorothy Thompson.

66   Nearly all his sketches in the magazine can be identified by a tiny stylized capital "H" in one corner of the picture.

67   Blanshard (1929), p. 2.

68   Hader, Elmer Stanley (1947).

69   Ibid., p. 13.

70   Ibid., pp. 16-17.

71   Ibid.

72   Hader, Elmer Stanley (1947).

73   Horner, Richard and Lynne Stuart (1981).

74   Hader, Elmer Stanley (1947).

75   "Francois Tonetti." "Mary Lawrence Tonetti." Wikipedia.

76   Hader, Elmer Stanley (1947), pp. 37-38.

77   Hader, Elmer Stanley (1947).

78   McBride (1969).

79   Holtz (1993).

80   Concordia University. Letter from Lynne Stuart to Gertrude Emerson Sen dated 2 March 1981.

81   Ibid. Letter from Eve Chappell to Lynne Stuart dated 24 July 1919.

82   McBride (1969).

83   University of Oregon. Marriage license of Elmer Hader and Berta Hoerner dated 14 July 1919.

84   Holtz (1993).

85   According to McBride (1969), many years later, when Berta was ripping out the dress to use for another project, she discovered Rose had used a little green thread to embroider "with love" in the seam.

86   McBride (1969).

87   Concordia University. Letter from Eve Chappel to Lynne Stuart dated 24 July 1919.

88   McBride (1969).

89   Hader, Elmer Stanley (1947), p. 48.

90   McBride (1969).

91   Hader, Elmer Stanley (1947), p. 49.

92   The Dutch called this spot on the Hudson "the Zee" or sea because it was so wide. Tappan came from the name of the Indians that once lived in the area.

93   Concordia University. "The Caliph in New York" by Charles Caldwell Dobie.

94   McBride (1969).

95   Ibid.

96   McBride (1949), p. 1412.

97   McBride (1959), p. 132.

98   University of Oregon. Letter by Elmer.

99   Bennett & Clark (1997).

100   McBride (1969).

101   "Haders Describe" (1936).

102   Ibid.

103   Hader, Elmer Stanley (1947), p. 53.

104   Ibid., p. 54.

105   Ibid.

106   Ibid.

107   Ibid., p. 60.

108   Porter (1977), p. 25.

109   Kemp (2009a).

110   Hader, Elmer Stanley (1947), p. 79.

111   Ibid., p. 80. The house was identified by Phippsburg Historian Jean Scott, Co-chair for Phippsburg's (Maine) Historic Preservation Commission and the family of Artist Ernest Haskell.

112   Hader, Elmer Stanley (1947), p. 75.

113   McBride (1959), p. 133.

114   Ibid.

115   Hader, Elmer Stanley (1947), p.102.

116   Ibid., p.83.

117   Apperson Jackrabbit. Wikipedia.

118   Hader, Elmer Stanley (1947), p. 90.

119   Ibid., p. 94.

120   Ibid.

121   Ibid.

122   Ibid., p. 102.

123   Flagg (2006).

124   Concordia University. Letter from Gertrude Emerson Sen to Lynne Stuart. India, 2 March 1981.

125   University of Oregon. Letter from Adelaide Gordon to Berta dated 18 May 1923.

126   University of Oregon. Letter from Elsie Weil to the Haders.

127   Hader, Elmer Stanley (1947), p. 113.

128   Ibid.

129   Savelle (1980), pp. 3M-4M.

130   McBride (1969).

131   Frowst means to lounge about in a stuffy atmosphere (*Online Oxford Dictionaries*).

132   University of Oregon. Letter from Elsie Weil to the Haders, Thanksgiving, 1925.

133   Kemp (2009a).

134   Concordia University. Letter from Jane Barrow to Lynne Stuart dated 25 March 1981.

135   Frederick O'Brien had asked Rose to edit his book on his travels in the Marquesa islands, and promised her an advance and royalties. He paid her the advance, but she never received any royalties, even when it became a best seller. Rose was bringing suit against him, but needed a contract to back her up.

136   Letter from Steve Kochersperger, Senior Research Analyst in Postal History, and Dr. Richard Kielbowicz, University of Washington, to Sybilla Avery Cook dated 29 April 2014.

137   Geist & Mathias (1968). The little girls were the Geist daughters.

138   Concordia University. Note from bank.

139   Lee (2007).

140   Pogany note.

141   Marcus (2008), p. 69.

142   Ibid., p. 71.

143   Lindbloom & Riley (1981).

144   Marcus (2008), p. 78.

145   Seaman (1928): 52-57.

146   Jean Stern, Executive Director, The Irvine Museum. "History of Plein Air Art." http://www.crystalcovebeachcottages.com.

147   Forry (2012).

148   *Horn Book* editor, post 1985.

149   Louise Seaman Bechtel saved many of these letters, not necessarily for the content but for the delightful sketches, and they are now in the archives at both Vassar College and the University of Florida.

150   Seaman (1928), p. 66.

151   Ibid.

152   University of Oregon.

153   University of Oregon. Letter to Hope Harshaw Evans dated 7 May 1970 regarding two picture books published by May Massie: *Monkey's Tale* (1929) and *Lion Cub* (1931).

154   University of Oregon. Elmer's letter dated 30 March 1929 to Ernestine Evans in reply to a letter from Coward McCann.

155   According to Holtz (1993), two of these were Rose Wilder Lane and Helen Boylston.

156 University of Oregon. Letter sent in 1931 to Eunice Blake: assistant editor to Seaman.

157 A new edition of this book was reproduced by Dover in 2014.

158 University of Oregon. Letter to Mr. McCann at Coward-McCann dated 8 June 1930.

159 Concordia University. Letter to Marian Webb of the Fort Wayne and Allen County, Indiana, Children's Department, 27 March 1964, answering a question about "the golden age" of the past.

160 Vasser College. Handcrafted holograph book from Berta and Elmer to Louise Seaman Bechtel.

161 Leota was Elmer's sister.

162 Dobbs (1949).

163 Vasser College. Handcrafted holograph book from Berta and Elmer to Louise Seaman Bechtel.

164 University of Oregon. Series of letters between Elmer and Knopf editor Marian Fiery.

165 Ibid.

166 Ibid.

167 University of Oregon. Based on Alfred A. Knopf letters.

168 Vassar College. Handcrafted holograph book from Berta and Elmer to Louise Seaman Bechtel.

169 The tips to three train porters totaled ninety-five cents.

170 University of Oregon. Letter from Houghton Mifflin to the Haders dated 12 April 1933.

171 Hader, Berta and Elmer (1933).

172 University of Southern Mississippi. Letter dated 12 September 1932 from W. F. Bigelow at *Good Housekeeping*.

173 Some of these maps have been recently reprinted, giving everyone the chance to compare their state in the 1930s with the one they live in today. The map of Maine is included in the *Historical Maine Atlas* published in December, 2014, by the University of Maine Press.

174 Royalties were still generous compared to today. A 1933 letter to the Haders from Houghton Mifflin offered "15% of net wholesale price to 5000 copies, 20% thereafter, with advance on publication based on advance sales."

175 Anderson (1981), pp. 437-440.

176 University of Oregon. Letter from Elmer to the Chamber of Commerce, Brownsville, Texas, dated 17 February 1934.

177 "Haders Describe" (1936).

178 "Leading" refers to the spacing between lines of type, which once was created by inserting blocks of lead.

179 "Haders Describe" (1936).

180 University of Oregon. Letter from Doris Patee to the Haders dated 9 December 1935.

181   "Haders Describe" (1936).

182   University of Oregon. Letter from Marion E. Merrill to the Haders dated 24 October 1934.

183   McBride (1949), p. 1413.

184   Panetta (2010).

185   "Woman Routs Surveyors" (1936).

186   "Rockland Women" (1936).

187   Panetta (2010).

188   The book has lasted, even though out of print. In 2011, it was highlighted in a blog by Summer Edwards, a children's literature specialist in Caribbean books, as giving an accurate glimpse into Jamaican life in the 1930s. "There is so much history to explore in both the text and the illustrations. Look at the way the characters are dressed! Look at the way the landscape is described in the text and depicted in the illustrations." (www.summeredwards.com)

189   University of Oregon. Correspondence from Doris Patee to the Haders.

190   "Haders Describe" (1936).

191   The book was sold for two dollars, according to the price printed on the first edition.

192   University of Oregon. Letter from Waldo Hader to the Haders dated 16 August 1935.

193   The original watercolor was sold at auction in 2001 for $63,250 according to Rich et al. (2013), p. 60.

194   Maine State Library. Letter from Hilda McLeod to the Haders dated 21 December 1937.

195   However, in 2010 the map of Maine was reprinted, and presented to Maine Senator Olivia Snowe. The newest version is now in the official Maine almanac. *Historical Atlas of Maine* (2014).

196   University of Oregon. Letter from Elmer dated 3 December 1936, responding to a request for a school visit.

197   McBride (1969).

198   Holtz (1993), p.152

199   Holtz (1993). Letter from William Holtz to Lynne Stuart.

200   Recollections from Joy Hoerner Rich during her visit to the Haders in 1941.

201   Dobbs (1949).

202   The "runner-up" designation was changed to "Honor Books" in 1981, and was made retroactive to the very beginning.

203   University of Oregon. Letter from Doris Patee to the Haders dated 7 January 1941.

204   Ibid.

205   University of Oregon. Letter from the Haders to Stanley J. Kunitz and Howard Haycroft, editors of *Twentieth Century Authors* dated 30 January 1940.

206   University of Oregon. Letter from Doris Patee to the Haders dated 7
      January 1941.

207   Ibid. Letter from Doris Patee to the Haders dated 30 October 1941.

208   The printers at Lithography-Typography-Review, Long Island.

209   Kemp (2009a). Letter from Jane Barrow.

210   Ware (2005).

211   University of Oregon. Letter from Doris Patee to the Haders dated 27
      January 1942.

212   University of Oregon. Letter from Jane Barrow to Lynne Stuart dated 1981.

213   University of Oregon. Letter from Berta to Jane Barrow dated 28 April
      1945.

214   "Anna and the King of Siam." Wikipedia.

215   Sahgal (1954).

216   Ibid.

217   University of Oregon. Susan Hirschman wrote a letter to the Haders dated
      4 June 1970, asking Berta & Elmer if they wanted to endorse the Lloyd
      Alexander statement for peace representing Publishers for Peace. Berta
      made a hand written notation on that letter "we telephoned 'Yes'."

218   University of Oregon. Letter from Doris Patee to the Haders dated 8 April
      1943.

219   University of Oregon. Letter from Berta to teacher Ada Randolph in
      Minnesota about their childhoods.

220   University of Oregon. Letter from Elsie Weil to the Haders dated 1943.

221   University of Oregon. Letter to Jane Barrow.

222   Letter from Patricia Carroll Compton to Karen Tolley dated 12 November 2014.

223   McBride (1949).

224   One observant child wrote the Haders that one of their snowflakes was
      wrong; it had only four sides.

225   McBride (1949), pp. 1412-1415.

226   Quack Quack, Macmillan, 1961. Also in Macmillan pamphlet on favorite authors.

227   Various letters to and from their friends refer to "Hader Haven," "Hader
      Heaven," "Hader Hovel," etc. depending on their mood.

228   University of Oregon. Letter to Doris Patee dated 10 February 1940 about
      the contract for Pancho.

229   The entire length of the bridge, with approaches, is 16,000 feet—nearly
      three miles.

230   The Herald Tribune (August 1953).

231   Panetta (2010), p. 59.

232   Geist & Mathias (1968), p. 9.

233   "Two Hudson Towns." (1954).

234   University of Oregon. Hand written draft of letter to Mrs. Eva S. Reeve at
      the Carnegie Library in Mitchell, South Dakota, dated February 1957.

235   Geist & Mathias (1968), p. 10.

236 Ibid., p. 10.

237 University of Oregon. Letter to Jane Barrow dated August 1950.

238 University of Oregon. Typed copy of a draft of *Working Together* by Berta & Elmer Hader.

239 McBride (1960), p.49.

240 Gies (1961), pp. 20, 23.

241 Sullivan (2003), p. 79.

242 Concordia University. Letter to Marian Webb of the Fort Wayne and Allen County, Indiana.

243 Burns (2002), p. 214.

244 University of Florida. Louise Seaman Bechtel, notes for speech. In her article she used the spelling and capitalization common in the 1600s, but I have adapted and simplified it for ease of reading.

245 Schulman (2008).

246 O'Donnell.

247 University of Oregon. Letter from Howard Applegate, Syracuse University, dated 23 August 1963, wishing to establish a Bertha (sic) Hader Manuscript Collection.

248 This is apparently an adaptation of verse VI of "Saul," a poem by Robert Browning. The original 1855 final version, can be found in *Browning's Complete Poetical Works.* Cambridge edition, Houghton Mifflin, Boston, 1895.

249 University of Oregon. Letters from Berta to Jane Barrow dated 1 July 1972.

250 The painting was cleaned and restored in 2012. It still hangs in the Wilder Historic Home and Museum at Rocky Ridge in Mansfield, Missouri.

251 Coward-McCann, Inc. advertisement in the Nyack (NY) *Journal,* [1934.]

252 University of Oregon. Letter accompanying the doll loaned to the Minneapolis Public Library, 1958.

253 University of Oregon. Letter from Rose Wilder Lane to Dorothy Thompson describing the furnishings.

254 Ibid.

255 Ibid. Anne Harris. "Thesis." Stetson Biography.

256 Ibid. Letter from Elmer to President Lyndon Johnson dated 9 February 1965.

257 Smaridge (1977), pp. 47-48.

258 Beman (1989a), p. 57.

259 University of Oregon. Letter to Hattie Bell Allen dated 12 August 1955.

260 Zoellner (2000).

BIBLIOGRAPHY

Adickes, Sandra E. 1991. *To Be Young Was Very Heaven: Women in New York Before the First World War.* New York: St. Martin's Press.

Anderson, William T. 1981. "How the 'Little House' books found a publishing home." *Language Arts* (April, 1981): 437-440.

"Artists Build their Own House." 1933. *Rocklander* (Sparkill, NY).

Bader, Barbara. 1976. *American Picture Books from Noah's Ark to the Beast Within.* New York: Macmillan.

Beatty, Bessie. 1919. *The Red Heart of Russia.* New York: Century Co.

Bechtel, Louise Seaman. 1969. *Books in Search of Children: Speeches and Essays by Louise Seaman Bechtel.* New York: Macmillan.

Beman, Lynn S. 1989a. *Elmer Stanley Hader. 1889-1973. A Rediscovered American Impressionist. His Life and Paintings. A Catalogue Raisonné.* Unpublished.

Beman, Lynn S. 1989b. *Elmer Stanley Hader. 1889-1973: Painter Rediscovered.* Exhibit Catalog. Paramus, NJ: Bergen Museum of Art and Science.

Beman, Lynn S. 1991. *Elmer Stanley Hader 1889-1973. Paintings.* Exhibit Catalog. Beverly Hills, CA: Louis Newman Galleries.

Bennett, Paula Pogany and Velma R. Clark. 1997. *The Art of Hungarian Cooking.* New York: Hippocrene Books.

Blanshard, Jill. 1929. "They're Married to their Art." *Times Herald*—Olean, NY (4 December 1929): 2.

Bodin, Walter. 1918. "Review." *San Francisco Bulletin* (April 20, 1918).

Burns, Mary Milham. 2002. "Picture Books." In Anita Silvey. *Essential Guide to Children's Books and Their Creators.* (Boston: Houghton Mifflin): 350-352.

Connelly, Marc. 1972. Forward to John Held. *The Most of John Held Jr.* (Brattlebors, VT: Stephen Greene Press).

Concordia University—Portland. Portland, Oregon. Hader Collection.

Dillon, Richard. 1985. *North Beach: the Italian Heart of San Francisco.* Novato, CA: Presidio Press.

Dobbs, Rose. 1949. "Personality into Books: Berta and Elmer Hader." *Horn Book* (November, 1949): 509-519.

Elleman, Barbara. 2002. *Virginia Lee Burton: A Life in Art.* Boston: Houghton Mifflin Harcourt.

Flagg, Ernest. 2006. *Flagg's Small Houses: Their Economic Design and Construction.* Mineola, NY: Dover Publications.

Forry, Timothy. "Revisiting A Few Early Berta and Elmer Hader Books." Blog: Childrens and Illustrated Books (Wednesday, 2 May 2012). http://childrensandillustratedbooks.blogspot.com/2012/05/revisiting-few-early-berta-and-elmer.html

Geist, Betty M. and Fred S. Mathias. 1968. *Grand View-on-Hudson: A History.* Grand View-on-Hudson: n.p.

Gies, Joseph. 1961. "Is Your Child a Victim of the Library Gap?" *This Week* (16 April 1961): 20, 23.

Gordon, Dick. 2011. Audiotape. The Story: "The Little Stone House." Interview with Joy Rich and Mark Goldstein. 21 January 2011. WUNC, North Carolina Public Radio. Distributed to National Public Radio by American Public Media.

Griffis, Enid. 1929. "Artists Grin at Temperament." *The Brooklyn Eagle Magazine* (16 November 1929): 13.

Hader, Berta and Elmer. 1933. "The Picture Book World: A Few Thoughts on the Subject." *School and Home* (January-March, 1933): 101-104.

Hader, Berta and Elmer. 1937. *Working Together.* New York: Macmillan.

Hader, Elmer. 1917. "Interview." *The Wasp: A Journal of Illustration and Comment* (3 November 1917): 12.

Hader, Elmer Stanley. 1917. *An Interview in the Mirror*. Unpublished manuscript.

Hader, Elmer Stanley. 1947. "Home is the Goal: An Idyll on the Hudson." Unpublished manuscript.

"Haders Describe How They Write Books for Children at Civic League Luncheon." 1936. *Nyack Daily News* (17 November 1936): 5.

Historical Atlas of Maine (2014). Orono: University of Maine Press.

Holtz, William. 1991. *Dorothy Thompson & Rose Wilder Lane: Forty Years of Friendship, Letters, 1921-1960*. Columbia: University of Missouri Press.

Holtz, William. 1993. *The Ghost in the Little House: A Life of Rose Wilder Lane*. Columbia: University of Missouri Press.

Hopkins, Lee Bennett. 1969. *Books Are By People.* New York: Citation Press.

Horner, Richard and Lynne Stuart. 1987. "Elmer Stanley Hader." Presentation at Village Hall in Grand View-on-Hudson, NY: 26 April 1987.

Horner, Richard and Lynne Stuart. 1981. "Working Together: The Story of Berta and Elmer Hader." Presentation at the Village Hall in Grand View-on-Hudson, NY: 24 May 1981.

Hughes, Edan Milton. 2002. *Artists in California, 1786-1940.* San Francisco: Crocker Art Museum.

Irwin, Wallace. 1904. "Telygraft Hill." *Sunset Magazine* (May 1904): 79.

Kemp, Edward and Elaine. 1977. "Berta and Elmer Hader of Willow Hill: A Hader Bibliography." *Imprint: Oregon.* Eugene: University of Oregon. Spring-Fall, 1977.

Kemp, Edward and Elaine. 2009a. "We Remember Berta and Elmer Hader." Presentation at the Multnomah County Library in Portland, Oregon. 27 January 2009.

Kemp, Edward and Elaine. 2009b. "Work Diary." Unpublished manuscript.

Lane, Rose Wilder. 1917. "Artist Brings Out Beauties of Landmark." *San Francisco Bulletin* (28 November – 12 December 1917).

Lee, Bill. 2007. "Berta and Elmer Hader and Their Little Stone House." Unpublished manuscript.

Lindbloom, Nancy Willard and Joyce Bickerstaff Riley. 1981. "Mr. Winkle Moves to Vassar." *Vassar Quarterly,* Spring-Summer.

Marcus, Leonard S. 1992. *Margaret Wise Brown: Awakened by the Moon*. New York: William Morrow.

Marcus, Leonard. 2002. *The Many Ways of Telling*. New York: Dutton.

Marcus, Leonard. 2008. *Minders of Make Believe*. New York: Houghton Mifflin.

McBride, Mary Margaret. "Elmer and Berta Hader, Winners of the Caldecott Medal." *Publishers' Weekly* (26 March 1949): 1412-1415.

McBride, Mary Margaret. 1959. *A Long Way from Missouri*. New York: Putnam.

McBride, Mary Margaret. 1960. *Out of the Air*. New York: Doubleday.

McBride, Mary Margaret. 1969. Audiotape Interviews with the Haders.

McBride, Mary Margaret and Alexander Williams. 1927. *Charm: A Book about It and Those Who Have It, For Those Who Want It*. New York: Rae D. Henkle.

McCorquedale, Duncan, Sophie Hallam, and Libby Waite. 2009. *Illustrated Children's Books*. London: Black Dog Publishing.

Meigs, Cornelia, Anne Theater Eaton, Elizabeth Nesbit, and Ruth Hill Viguers. 1953. *A Critical History of Children's Literature*. New York: Macmillan.

O'Donnell, Jr., Kevin. "How Thor Power Hammered Publishing." (www.sfwa.org/bulletin/articles.thor.htm)

Older, Mrs. Fremont. 1955. "Biography of Fremont Older." *San Francisco Call-Bulletin* (10 October 1955).

The Panama-Pacific International Exhibition. 2009. In *askART: The Artists Bluebook*. February, 2009.

Panetta, Roger. 2010. *The Tappan Zee Bridge and the Forging of the Rockland Suburb*. New City, NY: The Historical Society of Rockland County.

Parton, Margaret. 1945. *Laughter on the Hill: A San Francisco Interlude*. New York: McGraw-Hill.

Patee, Doris. 1937. *Berta and Elmer Hader: Working Together*. New York: Macmillan.

Patee, Doris. 1977. "Working Together. Berta and Elmer Hader. *Imprint: Oregon*. Eugene: University of Oregon.

Porter, Katherine Anne. 1977. *The Never-Ending Wrong*. New York: Little Brown & Co.

Rich, Joy Hoerner, Karen Tolley, John and Judy Waller. 2013. *Berta and Elmer Hader: A Lifetime in Art*. Roseburg, Oregon: Joyful Productions.

"Rockland Women Rout Bridge Aides." 1936. *The New York Times* (12 September 1936): 19.

Russell, John. 1989. "Art View." *The New York Times* (19 March 1989).

Sahgal, Nayantara Pandit. 1954. *Prison and Chocolate Cake*. New York: Knopf.

Savelle, Isabelle K. 1980. "The Village that Refuses to Die." *Journal News* (9 September 1980): 3M-4M.

Schulman, Janet. 2008. "Looking Back: The 1974 Macmillan Massacre." *Publishers Weekly* (10 April 2008).

Seaman, Louise. 1928. "Berta and Elmer and Their Picture Books." *Horn Book* (August, 1928): 52-57.

Smaridge, Norah. 1977. "Berta and Elmer Hader." In *Famous Literary Teams for Young People* (New York: Dodd, Mead): 43-48.

Sochen, June. 1972. *The New Woman: Feminism in Greenwich Village, 1910-1920.* New York: Quadrangle Books.

Stern, Jean. n.d. "History of Plein Air Art." (http://www.crystalcovebeachcottages.com/ resources/)

Stuart, Lynne. n.d. "Reflections on a Passing Cloud." Unpublished manuscript.

Sullivan, Peggy. 2003. "Fantasy Becomes Reality for School-Library Media Programs." *American Libraries* (March 2003): 79.

Taber, Louise E. 1917. "The Work of Elmer Stanley Hader: An Appreciation." San Francisco: Palace of Fine Arts.

Talley, Terry. 1989. *Oh What a Grand View: The Story of the Village of Grand-View-on-Hudson, New York.* Grand View-on-Hudson, NY: Beautification Committee.

Talley, Terry. 2006. *Gems on the Hudson: the Grand Views.* Tomkins Cove, NY: Magic Angel Books.

"Two Hudson Towns Rally to Bar Thruway Link." 1954. *New York Herald Tribune* (1 June 1954).

University of Florida. Gainesville, Florida. Louise Seaman Bechtel Collection.

University of Oregon. Eugene, Oregon. Hader Collection (AX441).

University of Southern Mississippi. Hattiesburg, Mississippi. DeGrummond Collection.

Vassar College. Poughkeepsie, New York. Louise Seaman Bechtel Collection.

Ware, Susan. 2005. *It's One O'clock and Here Is Mary Margaret McBride: A Radio Biography.* New York: New York University Press.

Wilder, Laura Ingalls and Almanzo Wilder. 1974. *West from Home: Letters of Laura Ingalls Wilder to Almanzo Wilder, San Francisco, 1915.* New York: Harper & Row.

"Woman Routs Surveyors for Hudson Bridge." 1936. *New York Herald Tribune* (12 September 1936).

Zoellner, Eleanor. 2000. "Letter to the Editor." In *South of the Mountains.* Rockland, NY: Rockland Historical Society.

BOOKS BY BERTA AND ELMER HADER

The following books, listed in chronological order, were illustrated by either or both Berta and Elmer Hader.

Boyce, Burke. *Stronghold*. 1927. (cover art only)

Hader, Berta and Elmer. *The Ugly Duckling*, 1927.

Hader, Berta and Elmer. *Chicken Little and the Little Half Chick*. 1927.

Hader, Berta and Elmer. *Hansel and Gretel*. 1927.

Hader, Berta and Elmer. *Wee Willie Winkie and Some Other Boys and Girls from Mother Goose*. 1927.

McBride, Mary Margaret and Alexander Williams. *Charm: A Book About It and Those Who Have It and Those Who Want It*. 1927.

Peedie, Jean Murdoch. *Donald in Numberland*. 1927.

Whitman, Chambers. *Don Coyote*. 1927. (cover art only)

Forgione, Louis. *The River Between*. 1928. (cover art only)

Hader, Berta and Elmer. *The Old Woman and the Crooked Sixpence*. 1928.

Hader, Berta and Elmer. *The Little Red Hen*. 1928.

Hader, Berta and Elmer. *The Picture Book of Travel: The Story of Transportation*. 1928.

Emerson, Edwin. *Adventures of Theodore Roosevelt*. 1928.

Livingston, Armstrong. *The Monk of Hambleton*. 1928. (cover art only)

Bentham, Josephine. *Bright Avenues*. 1928. (cover art only)

Bennet, Charles M. *Mutiny Island*. 1928. (cover art only)

Hader, Berta and Elmer. *The Story of the Three Bears*. 1928.

Meigs, Cornelia. *The Wonderful Locomotive*. 1928.

Hooker, Forrestine. *Garden of the Lost Key*. 1929.

Camp, Ruth Orton. *The Story of Markets*. 1929.

Holway, Frances Hope Kerr. *The Story of Water Supply*. 1929.

Hader, Berta and Elmer. *Two Funny Clowns*. 1929.

Williamson, Hamilton. A *Monkey Tale*. 1929.

Feuillet. Octave. *Story of Mr. Punch*. 1929.

Hader, Berta. *What'll You Do when You Grow Up?* 1929.

Baruch, Dorothy W. *Big Fellow at Work*. 1930.

Stoddard. Anne. *A Good Little Dog*. 1930.

Williamson, Hamilton. *Baby Bear*. 1930.

Williamson, Hamilton. *Little Elephant*. 1930.

Whitney, Elinor. *Timothy and the Blue Cart*. 1930.

Bigham, Madge Alford. *Sonny Elephant: A Jungle Tale*. 1930.

Hader, Berta and Elmer. *Lions and Tigers and Elephants Too: Being an Account of Polly Patchin's Trip to the Zoo.* 1930.

Hader, Berta and Elmer. *Under the Pignut Tree.* 1930.

Hader, Berta and Elmer. *Berta and Elmer Hader's Picture Book of Mother Goose.* 1930.

Hader, Berta and Elmer. *Summer under the Pignut Tree.* 1931.

Holway, Hope. *The Story of Health.* 1931.

Stoddard, Anne. *Bingo Is My Name.* 1931.

Hader, Berta and Elmer. *The Farmer in the Dell.* 1931.

Hader, Berta and Elmer. *Tooky: The Story of a Seal Who Joined the Circus.* 1931.

Williamson, Hamilton. *Lion Cub: A Jungle Tale.* 1931.

Hader, Berta and Elmer. *Berta and Elmer Hader's Picture Book of the States.* 1932.

Hahn, Julia Letheld. *Who Knows? A Little Primer.* 1932.

Stoddard, Anne. *Here Bingo.* 1932.

Lecky, Prescott. *Play-Book of Words.* 1933.

Hader, Berta and Elmer. *Chuck-A-Luck and His Reindeer.* 1933.

Hader, Berta and Elmer. *Spunky: The Story of a Little Shetland Pony.* 1933.

Hader, Berta and Elmer. *Whiffy Mcmann.* 1933.

Miller, Jane. *Jimmy the Groceryman.* 1934.

Hader, Berta and Elmer. *Midget and Bridget.* 1934.

Hahn, Julia Letheld. *Everyday Fun.* 1935.

Hader, Berta and Elmer. *Jamaica Johnny.* 1935.

Dalgliesh. Alice. *The Smiths and Rusty.* 1936.

Hader, Berta and Elmer. *Stop, Look, Listen.* 1936.

Hader, Berta and Elmer. *Billy Butter.* 1936.

Hader, Berta and Elmer. *Green and Gold: The Story of the Banana.* 1936.

Lee, Melicent Humason. *Marcos: A Mountain Boy of Mexico.* 1937.

Dalgliesh, Alice. *Wings for the Smiths.* 1937.

Moore, Clement. *A Visit from St. Nicholas.* 1937.

Lent, Henry Bolles. *The Farmer.* 1937.

Hader, Berta and Elmer. *Tommy Thatcher Goes to Sea.* 1937.

Hader, Berta and Elmer. *Working Together: The Inside Story of the Hader Books.* 1937.

Williamson, Hamilton. *Humpy: Son of the Sands.* 1937.

Steinbeck, John. *The Long Valley.* 1938. (cover art only)

Garrard, Phillis. *Banana Tree House.* 1938.

Hader, Berta and Elmer. *Cricket: The Story of a Little Circus Pony.* 1938.

Williamson, Hamilton. *Stripey, A Little Zebra.* 1939.

Steinbeck, John. *The Grapes of Wrath.* 1939. (cover art only)

Hahn, Julia Letheld. *Reading for Fun.* 1939.

Hader, Berta and Elmer. *Cock-A-Doodle-Doo: The Story of a Little Red Rooster.* 1939.

Thomas, Jean. *Ballad Makin' in the Mountains of Kentucky.* 1939. (cover art only)

Walmsley, Leo. *Love in the Sun.* 1939. (cover art only)

Rothermell, Fred. *The Ghostland.* 1940. (cover art only)

McBride, Mary Margaret. *How Dear to My Heart.* 1940.

Hader, Berta and Elmer. *The Cat and the Kitten.* 1940.

Hader, Berta and Elmer. *Little Town.* 1941.

Meller, Sidney. *Home Is Here.* 1941. (cover art only)

Gaggin, Eva Roe. *Down Ryton Water.* 1941.

Angelo, Valenti. *Hill of Little Miracles.* 1942. (cover art only)

Boyce, Burke. *The Perilous Night.* Viking Press, 1942. (cover art only)

Hader, Berta and Elmer. *The Story of Pancho and the Bull with the Crooked Tail.* 1942.

Hader, Berta and Elmer. *The Mighty Hunter.* 1943.

Mason, Miriam E. *Timothy Has Ideas.* 1943.

Hader, Berta and Elmer. *The Little Stone House: A Story of Building a House in the Country.* 1944.

Hader, Berta and Elmer. *Rainbow's End.* 1945.

Hader, Berta and Elmer. *Skyrocket.* 1946.

Hader, Berta and Elmer. *Big City.* 1947.

Bechtel, Louise Seaman. *Mr. Peck's Pets.* 1947.

Hader, Berta and Elmer. *The Big Snow.* 1948.

Singmaster, Elsie. *Isle of Que.* 1948.

Hader, Berta and Elmer. *Little Appaloosa.* 1949.

Hader, Berta and Elmer. *Squirrely of Willow Hill.* 1950.

Hader, Berta and Elmer. *Lost in the Zoo.* 1951.

Steinbeck, John. *East of Eden.* 1952. (cover art only)

Hader, Berta and Elmer. *Little White Foot: His Adventures on Willow Hill.* 1952.

Hader, Berta and Elmer. *The Friendly Phoebe.* 1953.

Hader, Berta and Elmer. *Wish on the Moon.* 1954.

Hader, Berta and Elmer. *Home on the Range: Jeremiah Jones & His Friend Little Bear in the Far West.* 1955.

Hader, Berta and Elmer. *The Runaways: A Tale of the Woodlands.* 1956.

Hader, Berta and Elmer. *Ding Dong Bell: Pussy's in the Well.* 1957.

Hader, Berta and Elmer. *Little Chip of Willow Hill.* 1958.

Hader, Berta and Elmer. *Reindeer Trail: A Long Journey from Lapland to Alaska.* 1959.

Hader, Berta and Elmer. *Mister Billy's Gun.* 1960.

Hader, Berta and Elmer. *Quack Quack: The Story of a Little Wild Duck.* 1961.

Steinbeck, John. *The Winter of Our Discontent.* 1961. (cover art only)

Hader, Berta and Elmer. *Little Antelope: An Indian for a Day.* 1962.

Hader, Berta and Elmer. *Snow in the City: A Winter's Tale.* 1963.

Hader, Berta and Elmer. *Two Is Company, Three's a Crowd: A Wild Goose Tale.* 1965.

Blair, Kathryn. *Barbary Moon.* 1970. (cover art only)

Barrow. Susan. *Mistress of Brown Furrows.* 1970. (cover art only)

Index

M

N

O

P

W

PRAISE FOR DRAWN TOGETHER

. . . an affectionate portrait of a marriage, a creative collaboration, and of a fateful interval in twentieth-century America's cultural coming of age.

Leonard S. Marcus, children's book historian, author, and critic

. . . an insightful and well-researched biography of Elmer and Berta Hader, the groundbreaking author-illustrator team whose work influenced generations of young readers.

Pamela Smith Hill, Laura Ingalls Wilder biographer

. . . the gift of an artistic couple – Berta and Elmer Hader – a history of children's literature, and a surprising connection to social change and the role of the arts within it, reminding us all of the power of children's art and literature to affect the world for good.

Jane Kirkpatrick, *New York Times* bestselling author of *A Light in the Wilderness*

. . . an extremely well-researched and readable biography exploring the lives of these two dedicated children's book creators and also some of the personalities of those who shaped the golden age of children's book illustration.

Anita Silvey, author of *Everything I Need to Know
I Learned from a Children's Book*

. . . a detailed and lively portrait of two distinguished pioneers of American picture books whose contribution to the field is indisputable and their books worth rediscovering.

Susan Hirschman, former editor for Macmillan

. . . a grand retelling of Elmer and Berta's love for each other, the lasting works they created together, and the home they built in Nyack, New York, which epitomized them and their love of nature.

Hilda K. Weisburg, editor & founder of School Librarian's Workshop

. . . a terrific dual biography that paints a portrait of a very special couple whose work changed the face of children's literature.

Barbara Swanson Sanders, children's literature consultant and educator

Photographer: Robert D. French

"SYBILLA! GET YOUR NOSE OUT OF THAT BOOK! RIGHT NOW."

Sybilla Cook was never been able to follow that rule. Her love of books and voracious reading began at an early age. She encouraged the same in her own children and became an active library volunteer at their school, involvement which led to becoming a librarian herself. After earning an M.A.L.S. from Dominican University, she served as a school librarian first in Illinois and later in Oregon. In 1986, the Oregon Educational Media Association gave her its first Oregon Elementary Library Media Teacher award, and she received several other reading and library awards for surrounding her students with interesting books and encouraging their love of reading.

Ms. Cook also earned an M.A. in Curriculum and Instruction from the University of Oregon, served as a consultant for several rural schools, and spent many years as an adjunct professor teaching in the library paraprofessional program at Western Oregon University. She has authored countless magazine and journal articles and two guidebooks about walking in Portland, Oregon, where she retired.

CPSIA information can be obtained
at www.ICGtesting.com
Printed in the USA
FSOW03n1358131116
27270FS